Sociology
A brief but critical introduction

SECOND EDITION

Anthony Giddens

palgrave
macmillan

First edition 1982
Second edition 1986

Published by
PALGRAVE MACMILLAN
Houndmills, Basingstoke, Hampshire RG21 6XS and
175 Fifth Avenue, New York, N.Y. 10010
Companies and representatives throughout the world

PALGRAVE MACMILLAN is the global academic imprint of the
Palgrave Macmillan division of St. Martin's Press, LLC and of
Palgrave Macmillan Ltd. Macmillan® is a registered trademark in
the United States, United Kingdom and other countries. Palgrave
is a registered trademark in the European Union and other
countries.

ISBN 0–333–42738–6 hardback
ISBN 0–333–42739–4 paperback

This book is printed on paper suitable for recycling and
made from fully managed and sustained forest sources.

A catalogue record for this book is available
from the British Library.

Printed and bound in Great Britain by
Biddles Ltd., King's Lynn, Norfolk

Contents

Preface

Over the past decade or so, major changes have taken place within sociology, and in the social sciences more generally. These developments, however, have for the most part been discussed only in literature of considerable complexity; they are not readily accessible to people lacking an acquaintance with the subject. I was prompted to write this book, therefore, in order to provide an introduction to sociology which reflects current developments, making them available to the beginning reader. I call the book a 'critical introduction' for two reasons. It is critical of a range of ideas that for a long period were the conventional wisdom of sociology. But I also claim that sociology, understood in the manner presented here, is necessarily directly linked to social criticism. Sociology cannot be a neutral intellectual endeavour, indifferent to the practical consequences of its analyses for those whose conduct forms its object of study.

This book differs from most other introductory texts in sociology in several ways. It incorporates a discussion of basic problems of social theory – the core of theoretical concerns which sociology shares with all the social sciences. I do not adopt the usual view that these issues are unimportant to those seeking to achieve an initial acquaintance with sociology. Neither do I accept the equally common idea that such matters are too complex to be grasped before the reader has a mastery of the more empirical content of the subject. In analysing this empirical content, I make certain emphases which diverge from those usually found in introductory works. Many accounts of sociology are written primarily with regard to one particular society – that in which the author, or the audience to which the book is directed, live. I try to avoid this type of parochialism, in the belief that one of the main tasks of sociological thought is to break free from the confines of the familiar. But perhaps the chief distinguishing feature of the book is its strongly historical stress. 'Sociology' and 'history' may be ordinarily taught as though they were distinct fields of study, but I think such a view to be mistaken.

I have tried to be concise, and this means some sacrifice in respect of comprehensiveness. I make no attempt to offer an encyclopaedic coverage of the whole range of topics that are legitimate areas of sociological interest. The reader wanting such a coverage must look elsewhere.

Anthony Giddens

Acknowledgements

The author and publishers wish to thank the following who have kindly given permission for the use of copyright material: The Controller of Her Majesty's Stationery Office for figure from *Social Trends*; United Nations for table from *United Nations Statistical Yearbook* (1981) © 1983. Every effort has been made to trace all the copyright-holders, but if any have been inadvertently overlooked the publishers will be pleased to make the necessary arrangement at the first opportunity.

1

Sociology: Issues and Problems

Sociology is a subject with a curiously mixed reputation. On the one hand, it is associated by many people with the fomenting of rebellion, a stimulus to revolt. Even though they may have only a vague notion of what topics are studied in sociology, they somehow associate sociology with subversion, with the shrill demands of unkempt student militants. On the other hand, quite a different view of the subject is often entertained – perhaps more commonly than the first – by individuals who have had some direct acquaintance with it in schools and universities. This is that in fact it is rather a dull and uninstructive enterprise, which far from propelling its students towards the barricades is more likely to bore them to death with platitudes. Sociology, in this guise, assumes the dry mantle of a science, but not one that proves as enlightening as the natural sciences upon which its practitioners wish to model it.

I think that those who have taken the second reaction to sociology have a good deal of right on their side. Sociology has been conceived of by many of its proponents – even the bulk of them – in such a way that commonplace assertions are disguised in a pseudo-scientific language. The conception that sociology belongs to the natural sciences, and hence should slavishly try to copy their procedures and objectives, is a mistaken one. Its lay critics, in some considerable degree at least, are quite correct to be sceptical of the attainments of sociology thus presented.

My intention in this book will be to associate sociology with the first type of view rather than the second. By this I do not mean to connect sociology with a sort of irrational lashing-out at all that most of the population hold to be good and proper ways of behaviour. But I do want to defend the view that sociology, understood in the manner in which I shall describe it, necessarily has a subversive quality. Its subversive or critical character, however, I shall argue, does not carry with it (or should not do so) the implication that it is an intellectually disreputable enterprise. On the contrary, it is exactly because sociology deals with problems of such pressing interest to us all (or should do so), problems which are the objects of major controversies and conflicts in society itself, that it has this character. However kempt or otherwise student radicals, or any other radicals, may be, there do exist broad connections between the impulses that stir them to action and a sociological awareness. This is not, or I imagine only very rarely, because sociologists directly preach revolt; it is because the study of sociology, appropriately understood, unavoidably demonstrates how fundamental are the social questions that have to be faced in today's world. Everyone is to some extent aware of these questions, but the study of sociology helps bring them into much sharper focus. Sociology cannot remain a purely academic subject, if 'academic' means a distinterested and remote scholarly pursuit, followed solely within the enclosed walls of the university.

Sociology is not a subject that comes neatly gift-wrapped, making no demands except that its contents be unpacked. Like all the social sciences – under which label one can also include, among other disciplines, anthropology, economics, and history – sociology is an inherently controversial endeavour. That is to say, it is characterised by continuing disputes about its very nature. But this is not a weakness, although it has seemed such to many of those who call themselves professional 'sociologists', and also to many others on the outside, who are distressed that there are numerous vying conceptions of how the subject-matter of sociology should be approached or analysed. Those who are upset by the persistent character of sociological debates, and a frequent lack of consensus about how to resolve them, usually feel that this is a sign of the immaturity of the subject. They want sociology to be like a natural science, and to generate a similar apparatus of universal laws to those which they see natural science as having discovered and validated. But according to the view I shall be outlining in this book, it is a mistake to suppose that sociology should be modelled too closely on the natural sciences, or to imagine that a natural science of society is either feasible or desirable. To say this, I should emphasise, does not mean that the methods and objectives of the natural sciences are wholly irrelevant to the study of human social behaviour. Sociology deals with a factually observable subject-matter, depends upon empirical research, and involves attempts to formulate theories and generalisations that will make sense of facts. But human beings are not the same as material objects in nature; studying our own behaviour is necessarily entirely different in some very important ways from studying natural phenomena.

The Context of Sociology

The development of sociology, and its current concerns,

have to be grasped in the context of changes that have created the modern world. We live in an age of massive social transformation. In the space of only something like two centuries a sweeping set of social changes, which have hastened rather than lessened their pace today, have occurred. These changes, emanating originally from Western Europe, are now global in their impact. They have all but totally dissolved the forms of social organisation in which humankind had lived for thousands of years of its previous history. Their core is to be found in what some have described as the 'two great revolutions' of eighteenth- and nineteenth-century Europe. The first is the French revolution of 1789, both a specific set of events and a symbol of political transformations in our era. For the 1789 revolution was quite different from rebellions of previous times. Peasants had sometimes rebelled against their feudal masters, for example, but generally in an attempt to remove specific individuals from power, or to secure reductions in prices or taxes. In the French revolution (to which we can bracket, with some reservations, the anti-colonial revolution in North America in 1776) for the first time in history there took place the overall dissolution of a social order by a movement guided by purely secular ideals – universal liberty and equality. If the ideals of the revolutionaries have scarcely been fully realised even now, they created a climate of political change that has proved one of the dynamic forces of contemporary history. There are few states in the world today that are not proclaimed by their rulers to be 'democracies', whatever their actual political complexion may be. This is something altogether novel in human history. It is true that there have been other republics, most especially those of Classical Greece and Rome. But these were themselves rare instances; and in each case those who formed the 'citizens' were a minority of the population, the majority of whom were slaves or others without the prerogatives of the select groups of citizenry.

The second 'great revolution' was the so-called 'industrial revolution', usually traced to Britain in the late eighteenth century, and spreading in the nineteenth century throughout Western Europe and the United States. The industrial revolution is sometimes presented merely as a set of technical innovations: especially the harnessing of steam power to manufacturing production and the introduction of novel forms of machinery activated by such sources of power. But these technical inventions were only part of a very much broader set of social and economic changes. The most important of these was the migration of the mass of the labour force from the land into the constantly expanding sectors of industrial work, a process which also eventually led to the widespread mechanisation of agrarian production. This same process promoted an expansion of cities upon a scale again previously unwitnessed in history. It has been calculated that prior to the nineteenth century, even in the most highly urbanised societies, no more than 10 per cent of the population lived in towns or cities – usually considerably less in most agrarian states and empires. By modern standards, virtually all cities in pre-industrial societies, even the most famed cosmopolitan centres, were relatively small. The population of London in the fourteenth century, for example, has been calculated at 30,000; that of Florence during the same period has been put at 90,000. By the turn of the nineteenth century, the population of London already outstripped that of any previous city in history, standing at some 900,000 souls. But in 1800, even with such a large metropolitan centre, only a small minority of the population of England and Wales lived in cities of any size. A century later, somewhere near 40 per cent of the population were inhabitants of cities of 100,000 or more, and nearly 60 per cent were living in cities of 20,000 or more.

TABLE 1.1 *Percentage of world's population living in cities*

	Cities of 20,000 or more	Cities of 100,000 or more
1800	2.4	1.7
1850	4.3	2.3
1900	9.2	5.5
1950	20.9	13.1
1970	31.2	16.7
1982	34.6	18.1

Source: Kingsley Davis, 'The origin and growth of urbanisation in the world', *American Journal of Sociology*, vol. 61, 1955 (updated).

Table 1.1 shows that urbanisation has expanded dramatically upon a world scale, and continues to do so. All the industrialised countries are highly urbanised, by whatever indices one chooses to distinguish the 'town' or 'city' from smaller population aggregates. But there are rapidly expanding urban areas in most of the Third World countries as well. The largest urban areas in the contemporary world are quite enormous when contrasted to cities in societies before the nineteenth century.

If industrialism and urbanism are at the heart of the transformations that have irretrievably dissolved most traditional forms of society, there is a third phenomenon associated with them which must be given mention. This is the quite staggering increase in the number of people in the world today, compared with yesteryear. It has been estimated that, at the time of the birth of Christ, the world probably contained something less than 300 million inhabitants. The total number seems to have grown at a fairly steady, but slow, rate up to the eighteenth century; world population probably just about doubled over this period. Since then there has occurred the 'population explosion' of which everyone has heard, however little they may know about the details. Today there are nearly 4,800 million people living in the world, this number expanding at such a rate that, if it continues, world population will double each forty years. While the consequences of such population growth for the future of humankind are fearful, and subject to considerable debate, the factors lying behind the origins of recent population growth are less controversial than those of industrialisation or urbanism. For most of human history, there has been a general balance between birth and death rates. While this in some respects is a complex matter, there are two main phenomena that dominate others. One is that, prior to the last two centuries, the average life span from birth was rarely more than thirty-five years, and often less. The second factor was the size of the mortality rate of children; it was not uncommon, in mediaeval Europe and elsewhere, for up to half of the children born annually to die before reaching adulthood. The rise in life expectancy, and dramatic decreases in child mortality rates – brought about by improved sanitation, general conditions of hygiene, and the medical conquest of some of the major infectious diseases – have unleashed this prodigious population growth.

Sociology: A Definition and Some Preliminary Considerations

Sociology came into being as those caught up in the initial series of changes brought about by the 'two great revolutions' in Europe sought to understand the conditions of their emergence, and their likely consequences. Of course, no field of study can be exactly pinpointed in terms of its origins. We can quite readily trace direct continuities from writers in the middle of the eighteenth century through to later periods of social thought. The climate of ideas involved in the formation of sociology in some part, in fact, helped *give rise* to the twin processes of revolution.

How should 'sociology' be defined? Let me begin with a banality. Sociology is concerned with the study of human societies. Now the notion of society can be formulated in only a very general way. For under the general category of 'societies' we want to include not only the industrialised countries, but large agrarian imperial states (such as the Roman Empire, or traditional China), and, at the other end of the scale, small tribal communities that may comprise only a tiny number of individuals.

A society is a cluster, or system, of *institutionalised* modes of conduct. To speak of 'institutionalised' forms of social conduct is to refer to modes of belief and behaviour that occur and recur – or, as the terminology of modern social theory would have it, are socially *reproduced* – across long spans of time and space. Language is an excellent example of such a form of institutionalised activity, or institution, since it is so fundamental to social life. All of us speak languages which none of us, as individuals, created, although we all use language creatively. But many other aspects of social life may be institutionalised: that is, become commonly adopted practices which persist in recognisably similar form across the generations. Hence we can speak of economic institutions, political institutions, and so on. Such a use of the concept 'institution', it should be pointed out, differs from the way in which the term is often employed in ordinary language, as a loose synonym for 'group' or 'collectivity' – as when, say, a prison or hospital is referred to as an 'institution'.

These considerations help to indicate how 'society' should be understood, but we cannot leave matters there. As an object of study, 'society' is shared by sociology and the other social sciences. The distinctive feature of sociology lies in its overriding concern with those forms of society that have emerged in the wake of the 'two great revolutions'. Such forms of society include those that are industrially advanced – the economically developed countries of the West, Japan and Eastern Europe – but also in the twentieth century a range of other societies stretched across the world. For no social order in modern times remains untouched by the forces unleashed by the 'two great revolutions'. I want to emphasise very strongly that the 'advanced' societies cannot be treated as though they were isolated from the rest of the world, or from societies that have preceded them in time – although a good deal of sociology is written as though such were the case.

In the light of these remarks, a definition can be offered of the subject as follows. *Sociology is a social science, having as its main focus the study of the social institutions brought into being by the industrial transformations of the past two or three centuries.* It is important to stress that there are no precisely defined divisions between sociology and other fields of intellectual endeavour in the social sciences. Neither is it desirable that there should be. Some questions of social theory, to do with how human behaviour and institutions should be conceptualised, are the shared concern of the social sciences as a whole. The different 'areas' of human behaviour that are covered by the various social sciences form an intellectual division of labour which can be justified in only a very general way.

Anthropology, for example, is concerned nominally with the 'simpler' societies: tribal societies, chiefdoms, and agrarian states. But these either have been dissolved altogether by the profound social changes that have swept through the world, or they are in the process of becoming incorporated within modern industrial states. The subject-matter of economics, to take another instance, is the production and distribution of material goods. However, economic institutions are plainly always connected with other institutions in social systems, which both influence and are influenced by them. Finally, history, as the study of the continual distancing of past and present, is the source material of the whole of the social sciences.

Many of the prominent thinkers associated with the development of sociology were impressed with the importance of science and technology in contributing to the changes they witnessed. In setting out the aims of sociology, therefore, they sought to duplicate, in the study of human social affairs, the successes of the natural sciences in explaining the material world. Sociology was to be a 'natural science of society'. Auguste Comte, who lived from 1798 to 1857, and who coined the term 'sociology', gave this view its clearest and most comprehensive formulation. All the sciences, he claimed, including sociology, share an overall framework of logic and method; all seek to uncover universal laws governing the particular phenomena with which they deal. If we discover the laws governing human society, Comte believed, we will be able to shape our own destiny in much the same way as science has allowed us to control events in the natural world. His famous formula, *Prévoir pour pouvoir* (to be able to predict is to be able to control), expresses this idea.

Since Comte's time, the notion that sociology should be fashioned upon the natural sciences has been the dominant view of the subject – although it has certainly not gone unchallenged, and has also been expressed in various differing ways. Emile Durkheim (1858–1917), one of the most influential figures in the development of sociology in the twentieth century, continued some of Comte's emphases. Sociology, he declared, is concerned with 'social facts', which can be approached in the same objective way as the facts with which the natural sciences deal. In his short, but very influential book *The Rules of Sociological Method* (1895), Durkheim proposed that social phenomena should be treated like *things*: we should regard ourselves as though we were objects in nature. Thereby he accentuated the similarities between sociology and natural science.

As I have mentioned earlier, although this type of standpoint has been very pervasive in sociology, it is one I reject. To speak of sociology, and of other subjects like anthropology or economics, as 'social sciences', is to stress that they involve the systematic study of an empirical subject-matter. The terminology is not confusing so long as we see that sociology and other social sciences differ from the natural sciences in two essential respects.

(1) We *cannot* approach society, or 'social facts', as we do objects or events in the natural world, because societies only exist in so far as they are created and re-created in our own actions as human beings. In social theory, we cannot treat human activities as though they were determined by causes in the same way as natural events are. We have to grasp what I would call the *double involvement* of individuals and institutions: we create society at the same time as we are created by it. Institutions, I have said, are patterns of social activity reproduced across time and space. It is worthwhile reflecting for a moment upon what this involves. To speak of the 'reproduction' of social conduct or social systems

is to speak of the *repetition* of similar patterns of activity by actors separated from each other in time and space. It is very important indeed to stress this point, because much social theory – including that of Durkheim – is pervaded by a tendency to think in terms of physical imagery, a tendency which can have damaging consequences. Social systems involve patterns of relationships among individuals and groups. Many sociologists picture these patterns as rather like the walls of a building, or the skeleton of a body. This is misleading because it implies too static or unchanging an image of what societies are like: because it does not indicate that the patterning of social systems only exists in so far as individuals actively repeat particular forms of conduct from one time and place to another. If we were to use this sort of imagery at all, we should have to say that *social systems are like buildings that are at every moment constantly being reconstructed by the very bricks that compose them.*

(2) It follows from this that the practical implications of sociology are not directly parallel to the technological uses of science, and cannot be. Atoms cannot get to know what scientists say about them, or change their behaviour in the light of that knowledge. Human beings can do so. Thus the relation between sociology and its 'subject-matter' is necessarily different from that involved in the natural sciences. If we regard social activity as a mechanical set of events, determined by natural laws, we both misunderstand the past and fail to grasp how sociological analysis can help influence our possible future. As human beings, we do not just live in history; our understanding of history is an integral part of what that history is, and what it may become. This is why we cannot be content with Comte's idea of *Prévoir pour pouvoir*, seen as social technology. In the social sciences, we are addressing other human beings, not an inert world of objects. It is often

precisely by showing that what may appear to those involved as inevitable, as unchallengeable – as resembling a law of nature – is, in fact, an historical product, that sociological analysis can play an emancipatory role in human society. At the same time, sociological analysis teaches sobriety. For although knowledge may be an important adjunct to power, it is not the same as power. And our knowledge of history is always tentative and incomplete.

The Sociological Imagination: Sociology as Critique

The practice of sociology, I argue in this book, demands invoking what C. Wright Mills has aptly called the 'sociological imagination' (C. Wright Mills, *The Sociological Imagination*, Harmondsworth, Penguin, 1970). The term has been so oft-quoted that it is in danger of being trivialised, and Mills himself used it in a rather vague sense. I mean by it several related forms of sensibility indispensable to sociological analysis as I conceive of it. An understanding of the social world initiated by the contemporary industrialised societies – present-day society as first formed in the West – can only be achieved by virtue of a threefold exercise of the imagination. These forms of the sociological imagination involve an *historical*, an *anthropological*, and a *critical* sensitivity.

Human beings, genetically identical to us, have probably existed for something like 100,000 years. So far as we know from archaeological remains, 'civilisations', based upon settled agriculture, have been in existence at the most for only the past 8,000 years. But this seems a very large period of time compared with the tiny sliver of recent history dominated by the rise of industrial capitalism. Historians are not agreed about dating the origins of

Western capitalism as a prevailing mode of economic enterprise; but it is difficult to make a case for placing it further back than the fifteenth or sixteenth centuries in Europe. Industrial capitalism, the conjunction of capitalistic enterprise with machine production in the factory, has its origins no earlier than the latter part of the eighteenth century, and then was to be found only in parts of Britain. The past hundred years, the century or so which has seen the world-wide expansion of industrial capitalism, have none the less brought about social changes more shattering in their consequences than any other period in the whole previous history of humankind. Those of us in the West live in societies that have absorbed the first impact of these changes. The contemporary generation is familiar with societies geared to rapid technological innovation, in which most of the population live in towns or cities, work in industrial labour, and are 'citizens' of nation-states. But this now familiar social world, created so rapidly and dramatically in such a brief time span, is quite unique in human history.

The first effort of sociological imagination that has to be exercised by the analyst of the industrialised societies today is that of recovering our own immediate past – the 'world we have lost'. Only by such an effort of the imagination, which of course involves an awareness of history, can we grasp just how differently those in the industrialised societies live today from the way people lived in the relatively recent past. Brute facts help, such as those I mentioned in connection with urbanism. But what is really demanded is an attempt at the imaginative reconstruction of the texture of forms of social life that have now been very largely eradicated. Here there is no distinction between the craft of the sociologist and the art of the historian. Eighteenth-century Britain, the society in which the impact of the industrial revolution was first experienced, was still a society in which the customs of the local community held sway, knit together by the pervading influence of religion. It was a society in which we can see recognisable continuities with Britain in the twentieth century, but where the contrasts are quite remarkable. The organisations which are so commonplace today existed in no more than rudimentary form: not just factories and offices, but schools, colleges, hospitals, and prisons only came to be widespread in the nineteenth century.

These changes in the texture of social life are of course in some part of a material sort. As one historian describing the industrial revolution has written:

> Modern technology produces not only more, faster; it turns out objects that could not have been produced under any circumstances by the craft methods of yesterday. The best Indian hand spinner could not turn out yarn so fine and regular as that of the mule; all the forges in eighteenth-century Christendom could not have produced steel sheets so large, smooth, and homogeneous as those of a modern strip mill. Most important, modern technology has created things that could scarcely have been conceived in the pre-industrial era: the camera, the motor car, the aeroplane, the whole array of electronic devices from the radio to the high-speed computer, the nuclear power plant, and so on almost *ad infinitum* . . . The result has been an enormous increase in the output and variety of goods and services, and this alone has changed man's way of life more than anything since the discovery of fire: the Englishman of 1750 was closer in material things to Caesar's legionnaires than to his own great-grand-children. (David S. Landes, *The Unbound Prometheus*, Cambridge, Cambridge University Press, 1969, p. 5.)

The sheer scale and pervasive character of technological innovation is indeniably one of the distinctive features of the industrialised societies today. Closely connected to it is the decline of tradition, the foundation of day-to-day life in the local village community and important even in urban life in the pre-capitalist era. Tradition encapsulated the present in the past, and implied an experience of time distinct from that which predominates in contemporary Western societies. The individual's day was not demarcated into 'work time' and 'free time' as tends to be the case today; and 'work' was not cleanly separated from other activities, either in time or in space.

I referred earlier to the intersection of two great revolutions that lie at the origin of the transformation of the societies of Western Europe. The second was political revolution, which connects to the rise of the nation-state, as significant a phenomenon as the rise of industrialism in creating the modern world. Those living in the West tend to take it for granted that they are all 'citizens' of a particular nation, and no one could fail to be aware of the extensive part which the state (centralised government and local administration) plays in their lives. But the development of rights of citizenship, in particular the universal franchise, is also relatively recent. So is nationalism, the feeling of belonging to a distinctive national community, separate from others. These have become characteristic features of the 'internal' organisation of nation-states, but it is equally important to draw attention to the relations *among* nation-states as fundamentally distinctive of the modern era.

We live today in a world system that has no parallel in previous ages. The 'two great revolutions' have each proved to have ramifications on a world scale. Industrial capitalism is predicated upon an enormously complicated specialisation of production, a division of labour in which exchange relationships are world-wide. Consider the clothes you are wearing, the room in which you are sitting, or the food you will eat at your next mealtime. It is unlikely that you yourself will have made your own clothing, constructed your own dwelling, or grown the food you consume. In the industralised countries we are quite accustomed to such a situation, but before the advent of industrial capitalism the division of labour was very much less complex. The majority of the population catered directly for most of their own needs, and where they did not they drew upon the services of others in their local community. But today products are manufactured and exchanged world-wide, in a truly global division of labour. Not only are many of the goods consumed in the West produced on the other side of the world, and to some extent vice versa, but there may be intricate connections among productive processes carried on in widely separated places. Some parts of a TV set, for example, might be made in one country, other parts elsewhere; the set might then be assembled somewhere else, and be sold in yet another place altogether.

But it is not only the expansion of economic relationships that has given rise to a novel and unique world system. The spread of capitalism has been accompanied by the general prevalence of the nation-state. I have mentioned some of the 'internal' characteristics of the nation-state (and will analyse these more fully in Chapter 7). In an important sense, however, it is misleading to speak of 'the' nation-state, because from their early origins in Europe there have always been nation-*states*, existing in mixed relations of harmony and conflict with one another. Today the whole world is divided into a patchwork of nation-states. Both the emergence of nation-states in Europe, and especially their development in other parts of the world are, once more, relatively recent phenomena. For most of its history, humankind has been thinly scattered throughout the world, living in very small societies, and existing by hunting animals and gathering edible plants – so-called 'hunting and gathering' societies. Over most of the past ten or so millennia, the world was still only sparsely populated, compared with today, by people living either in hunting and gathering societies, small agricultural communities, city-states, or empires. Some empires, most notably that of China, have been very large. But they were quite different in form from contemporary nation-states. The central Chinese government in traditional China, for example, never managed to achieve much direct control over its various provinces, especially the more far-flung ones. Most of those subject to the rule of the Chinese state lived lives utterly different from those of their rulers, with whom they had little in common with respect to either culture or language.

Moreover, although the various types of society just mentioned existed in various sorts of relationship with one another, those connections certainly did not span the globe as they do today. The observation 'East is East and West is West, and ne'er the twain shall meet', prior to the present century, expressed a very real circumstance. There were sporadic contacts, and a certain amount of intermittent trade, between China and Europe from the eleventh century onwards; but for centuries afterwards China and the West to all intents and purposes inhabited separate universes from one another. Today all this has changed, whatever cultural differences might still separate East and West. China is no longer an empire but a nation-state, albeit one of massive dimensions in terms of both territory and population. It is, of course, also a self-professedly socialist state; although nation states now span the world, they have by no means all followed the 'liberal-democratic' model that has been most firmly established in Western Europe.

If the first dimension of the sociological imagination involves the development of an historical sensibility, the second entails the cultivation of anthropological insight. To say this is again to emphasise the tenuous nature of the conventionally recognised boundaries among the various social sciences. The fostering of an historical sense of how recent and how dramatic are the social transformations of the past two centuries is difficult. But it is perhaps even more challenging to break away from the belief, explicit or implicit, that the modes of life which have developed in the West are somehow superior to those of other cultures. Such a belief is encouraged by the very spread of Western capitalism itself, which has set in motion a train of events that has corroded or destroyed most other cultures with which it has come into contact. Moreover, many social thinkers have given concrete form to this notion in attempting to squeeze human history into schemes of social evolution, in which 'evolution' is understood in terms of the capability of varying types of society to control or master their material environments. Western industrialism inevitably appears at the apex of these schemes, since it has undeniably unleashed a material productivity vastly greater than that of any other societies which have preceded it in history.

Such evolutionary schemes, however, express an ethnocentrism which it is the task of the sociological imagination to dispell. An ethnocentric conception is one that takes the standpoint of one's own society or culture as a measure to judge all others. There is no doubt that such an attitude has been deeply entrenched in Western culture. It has also been characteristic of many other societies. However, in the West a conviction of superiority has been in some part an expression, and a justification, of the greedy engulfing of other modes of life by industria capitalism. But we must not confuse the economic and military power of the Western societies, which has allowed them to assume a pre-eminent position in the world, with the highpoint of an evolutionary scheme. The valuation of material productivity that is so pronounced in the modern West is itself a specifically anomalous attitude when compared with other cultures.

The anthropological dimension of the sociologica imagination is important because it allows us to appreci ate the diversity of modes of human existence which have been followed on this earth. It is one of the ironies of the modern era that the systematic study of the diversity of human cultures – 'field-work anthropology' – came into being at the very time when the voracious expansion of industrial capitalism and Western military power was accelerating their destruction. But the anthropologica aspect of the sociological imagination has featured in the social sciences from their inception, vying with evolutionary thought of an ethnocentric character. In Jean-Jacques Rousseau's *Discourse on the Origin and Foundation of Inequality* (1755) we find an illuminating insistence upon the idea that, through becoming aware of the dazzling variety of human societies, we can learn better to understand ourselves. 'The whole world. Rousseau remarked, is covered with societies 'of which we know only the names, yet we dabble in judging the human race!' Imagine, he continued, that we were able to send out an intrepid band of observers sensitive to the diversity of human experience to describe the multifariou societies which exist, but about which we know little. 'Le us suppose,' he wrote, 'that these new Hercules, back from these memorable expeditions, then wrote at leisure the natural, moral, and political history of what the would have seen; we ourselves would see a new work come from their pens, and we would thus learn to know our own.'

In the century and a half that followed the publication of Rousseau's *Discourse*, travellers, missionaries, traders, and others did make many of these journeys. But the reports they rendered were frequently unreliable or partial, or embodied the very ethnocentrism which Rousseau wanted to attack. Anthropological field-work of a systematic and detailed kind only began at about the turn of the twentieth century. Since that time, within a rapidly diminishing universe of study, anthropologists have accumulated a large body of information about different cultures. This information does, on the one hand, confirm the unity of the human race; there are no grounds for holding that people living in small, 'primitive' societies are in any way genetically inferior to or different from those living in supposedly more advanced 'civilisations'. There are no known human societies without developed forms of language, and there seems to be no correlation between types of society and linguistic complexity. On the other hand, modern anthropological research also underlines the wide spectrum of institutions whereby human beings may order their lives.

Often, the contemporary anthropologist is a chronicler of disaster, or culture laid waste by military destruction, ravaged by illness introduced by contact with the West, or undermined by the dissolution of traditional customs. The anthropologist is, as Claude Lévi-Strauss, perhaps the most distinguished practitioner of the subject in the world today, has put it, the 'pupil and the witness' of these disappearing peoples. There are urgent and very practical issues involved in the fight to block the continuing despoiling of the rights of such peoples, or at least to smooth their adjustment to new modes of life where their own have already crumbled. But the significance of such

struggles should not lead us to ignore the importance o
the anthropological work that has been produced ove:
the past half-century or so; from such work we can keep
alive in our thinking forms of social life that may be or
the verge of being eradicated for ever.

Combining this second sense with the first, the exercise
of the sociological imagination makes it possible to break
free from the straitjacket of thinking only in terms o
the type of society we know in the here and now. Each i:
thus directly relevant to the third form of the sociologica
imagination that I want to point to. This concerns the
possibilities for the future. In criticising the idea that
sociology is like a natural science, I have insisted that no
social processes are governed by unalterable laws. A:
human beings, we are not condemned to be swept along
by forces that have the inevitability of laws of nature
But this means we must be conscious of the *alternative*
futures that are potentially open to us. In its third sense
the sociological imagination fuses with the task o
sociology in contributing to *the critique of existing form*
of society.

Critique must be based on analysis. In the following
chapters, I shall begin by discussing different views of the
nature of the industrialised societies, contrasting riva
interpretations. But the changes initiated in the West, a
I have stressed previously, cannot be grasped withou
looking at the relations between those societies and th
rest of the world. Hence I shall subsequently discuss, ii
some detail, the significance of the formation of th
contemporary world system, a phenomenon fundamenta
to assessing the future potentialities of human socia
organisation.

2

Competing Interpretations: Industrial Society or Capitalism?

How are we to interpret the consequences of the 'two great revolutions' for subsequent development of the industrialised sectors of the world? While a range of analyses of the origins and character of the industrialised societies have been developed in sociology, there is one major line of division around which different views tend to cluster, and it is this division that I shall concentrate upon in this chapter. I have earlier used the terms 'industrialised societies' or 'industrial capitalism' to characterise the type of society that emerged in the late eighteenth and nineteenth centuries in Western Europe. I shall continue to employ these terms in the remainder of the book, but at this juncture it is necessary to point to some terminological contrasts that are very important for the problems I want to discuss and the issues I shall pose.

I shall want to distinguish what I shall call the theory of *industrial society*, on the one hand, from the theory of *capitalist society*, on the other. These two terms are not innocent labels, but call attention to two contrasting ways in which social thinkers have tried to understand the nature of the changes that have transformed the modern

world. The term 'industrial society' was coined by Comte
Henri de Saint-Simon, writing in the early years of the
nineteenth century, and he also established some general
theoretical guidelines that were later taken up by others.
Among these later authors was Durkheim, whose
influence upon sociology has by no means been solely a
methodological one. Durkheim did not actually favour
the term 'industrial society', but he gave a comprehensive
statement of the sort of standpoint I have in mind. The
theory of industrial society was given a new impetus in
the 1950s and 1960s, at the hands of a number of
prominent authors in Europe and the United States.
Indeed, it became something of an orthodoxy at that
period.

The conception of capitalist society is associated above
all with Karl Marx, although Marx appropriated some of
his main ideas from various preceding schools of thought in
social theory, philosophy, and economics. Marx produced
the majority of his most important works between 1840
and 1870. In his own lifetime (1818–83), these writings
were well known to only a fairly small number of associates
and followers. But as Marxist political movements, and
labour movements more generally, became more powerful
in the latter decades of the nineteenth century, Marx's
ideas came to be the subject of numerous debates and
controversies – and have remained so ever since. However,
they have also undergone continual development since
Marx's time; today Marxism represents an internally
diverse body of thought, and in the short compass of this
book I shall be able to discuss only a few major themes
in this now abundant literature. Perhaps at this point I
should already declare *parti pris*. I shall want to argue that
Marx's writings are of continuing significance to sociology,
and that they are the main basis from which some of the
suppositions of the theory of industrial society have to

be criticised. At the same time, however, there are conspicuous weaknesses in Marx's work that cannot be ignored.

The Theory of Industrial Society

In introducing the theory of industrial society, and contrasting it with views expressed by, or derived from, Marx, I have to make some initial qualifications. The contrasts that I shall draw, and the threads of discussion I shall follow, in no way exhaust the modes in which sociological ideas can be categorised. If Marxism comprises a variegated set of approaches, the variety of forms of non-Marxist social thought is very considerably greater. A certain amount of simplification of what are often rather complex problems is therefore unavoidable; and inevitably I shall have to ignore some questions and ideas which in a longer work would merit direct consideration.

The comparisons I make between the two perspectives below, therefore, are given by way of setting the scene. This is not a 'Marxist' book; to declare sympathy with certain of Marx's conceptions does not imply accepting his views, or those of any of his self-professed followers, in their entirety. But neither do I reject Marx in favour of the theory of industrial society. We have something to learn from both standpoints. Each has defined limitations, which we have to seek to identify and then improve upon. You will often find authors who will insist that 'Marxism' and so-called 'bourgeois sociology' are incompatible, and hence that one must opt for one at the expense of the other. But that is not my view.

The notion of 'industrial society', as I have mentioned, can be traced back to Saint-Simon. There are, I think, continuities between Saint-Simon's ideas and those of much more recent thinkers. But by the 'theory of industrial society' I do not mean to refer to a precise set of axioms shared by a specific school of thinkers. Rather, I refer to a number of concepts and interpretations that have tended generally to cluster together. Different authors have emphasised certain of these at the expense of others, and have expressed the ideas involved at varying levels of sophistication and subtlety. (A helpful survey of these ideas appears in Krishan Kumar, *Prophecy and Progress*, London, Allen Lane, 1978.)

Those thinkers whom I would link to the theory of industrial society have advocated at least some among the following notions.

(1) The most significant set of changes to be found in the contemporary world is to do with the transition from 'traditional' societies, based primarily upon agriculture, on the one hand, to 'industrial societies', based upon mechanised production and exchange of goods, on the other. Writers have used various labels to refer to these two types of society, and have characterised the traditional and industrial types in differing ways. Also they have recognised that 'tradition' and 'modernity' may combine in varying fashion in different countries.

(2) The transition from traditional to industrial society represents a progressive movement in history. No one, of course, pretends that industrial societies are lacking in conflicts or tensions. But these tend to be counterbalanced, it is argued, by the beneficent features of the industrial order, which both generates material affluence and is associated with the dissolution of traditional constraints. An industrial society is one in which rigid forms of social distinction – such as those between aristocrats or gentry and the 'common people' – become dissolved. It is a society in which equality of opportunity tends to prevail.

(3) The class conflicts witnessed in Western Europe in the nineteenth and early twentieth centuries are explained as a result of the strains involved in the transition from an agrarian order to an industrial society. The most influential notion here is often referred to as the 'institutionalisation of class conflict'. In the early origins of the newly emerging industrial society, class divisions were acute, and class relations were the focus of major tensions. But these tensions have been largely dispelled as accepted modes of industrial bargaining became established, in conjunction with the extension of 'political citizenship rights' – the right to vote and to form political parties – to include the mass of the population. (An influential analysis along these lines, which remains of considerable interest today, is Seymour Martin Lipset, *Political Man*, New York, Doubleday, 1960.)

(4) The rise of the liberal-democratic state is an essential element accompanying the transition from tradition to modernity. A liberal democracy is a political system, of the sort familiar in Western Europe and the United States, in which parliamentary government prevails, and in which two or more parties vie for the favour of the electorate. Many authors have tended to suppose that this form of state is something of a natural accompaniment to the expansion of industrial societies. Others have been more acutely aware of its distinctive properties, and have criticised such a standpoint, arguing that the modern state has played a fundamental role in social change in its own right (see Reinhard Bendix, *Nation-Building and Citizenship*, New York, Wiley, 1964).

(5) Proponents of the theory of industrial society have tended to presume, or to propose, that there is an essential unity to the industrial order wherever it emerges. Sometimes this idea has been stated in a peculiarly blunt form, most notably by Kerr and his colleagues (Clark Kerr

et al., *Industrialism and Industrial Man*, Harmondsworth, Penguin, 1973). According to Kerr's 'convergence theory', there is what he calls a 'logic of industrialism' which inexorably leads industrial societies to become increasingly alike in their basic institutions, however different they may have been originally. The more highly industrialised societies are, the more they tend to resemble one another, as the remnants of tradition are swept away. Kerr concentrated his attention mainly upon the United States and the Soviet Union, claiming that, in spite of their divergences in political ideology, the two societies were coming to converge upon a common path of development. This kind of conception still commands some adherents. It has also been strongly criticised, however – by those like Bendix, for example, who emphasise the varying ways in which tradition and modernity are intermingled in contemporary societies.

Such critics, none the less, still often consider that industrial or 'modernised' societies have definite overall similarities, whatever differences may also be observed among them. Moreover, they hold that such overall characteristics of industrial societies are necessary features of them, precluding their possible radical transformation. These views may not, as in the case of Kerr and others, involve a technological determinism. Many writers, for example, have taken their cue from the writings of Max Weber (1864–1920), arguing that *large-scale organisation* is a necessary feature of contemporary societies, and that this has certain universal features. Like Max Weber, they are usually directly critical not only of Marxism but also of the ideals of socialism more generally. I shall explain their reasons for taking such a viewpoint at a later point in this chapter, since they are of some considerable importance to social thought. (See also below, pp. 84–6.)

(6) The conception of industrial society has often been

closely associated with so-called 'modernisation theory' in respect of non-industrialised societies in the world. The idea of modernisation tends to mesh rather readily with the other suppositions and themes I have mentioned above. The key idea in modernisation theory is that the 'underdeveloped' societies remain trapped within traditional institutions, from which they have to break free if they are to approach the economic prosperity achieved in the West. This perspective has again been formulated with lesser and greater degrees of sophistication. Sometimes 'modernisation' simply means 'Westernisation', an elision that is very easy to make if one presumes that all industrial societies are basically alike. Most writers, however, recognise that 'industrial society' incorporates institutions originally formed within Western culture, and that other societies on the road to industrialisation will differ in some ways from the West. At the same time, they hold that 'underdevelopment' can only be overcome by the adoption of modes of behaviour based upon those found in the existing industrialised societies. I shall discuss issues raised by this sort of standpoint in Chapter 7.

My remarks so far have all been on a rather abstract plane, and it will help to make matters more concrete. A useful way to do this is to outline a particular version of the theory of industrial society, subsequently comparing it with a Marxist interpretation. An influential account which fits the bill neatly is that offered by Ralf Dahrendorf in his book *Class and Class Conflict in Industrial Society* (Stanford, Stanford University Press, 1959 [original German publication 1957]). Although the work first appeared some while ago, and its author has himself subsequently revised some of the views set out in it, it contains ideas which remain in wide currency. Moreover, the work was penned explicitly as a critical discussion of

Marx, and therefore lends itself readily to comparison with a standpoint of a more explicitly Marxist kind.

Dahrendorf begins his account by directly comparing the relative usefulness of the concepts of 'industrial' and 'capitalist' society. While the latter was used by Marx, Dahrendorf makes a case for claiming that the former is to be preferred as a more inclusive term for understanding the Western societies. 'Industrial production,' Dahrendorf avers, 'is not just a passing guest in history, but probably will be with us forever in one form or another' (Dahrendorf, p. 40). 'Industrialisation', as he uses the term, refers to the mechanised production of goods in factories or other enterprises; an industrial society is one in which industrialism is the prevalent form of economic organisation.

Dahrendorf leaves us in no doubt that industrialisation is the principal phenomenon influencing the development of the contemporary societies. Capitalism, he says, is only one mode of organising an industrial society – a transitory form, limited to the Western European societies in the nineteenth and early twentieth centuries. A capitalist society, in his view, is one in which industrial production lies primarily in private hands: in which the industrial entrepreneur is at once the owner of a factory or factories, and the chief directive authority over the workers. But this coincidence of industrial ownership and control proved to be only a short-lived phenomenon. With the increasing scale of industry since Marx's day, the ownership of capital no longer confers control over the authority system of the enterprise. (The classic statement of this view is to be found in A. A. Berle and G. C. Means, *The Modern Corporation and Private Property*, New York, Collier-Macmillan, 1968 [originally published 1932].) Those who control industrial production today, especially in the large firms which come increasingly to predominate in the economy, are managerial executives. Marx (I shall discuss this below) regarded private ownership of capital as the prime feature of capitalism. In this, however, Dahrendorf argues, he was mistaken. Capitalism, as contrasted to industrialism, has indeed proved to be 'a passing guest in history'. Capitalist society is but one sub-type of industrial society, really little more than a phase in the development of industrial society.

In a certain sense there is agreement here between Dahrendorf and Marx; each holds that capitalism is a type of society destined to be supplanted by another. But the way in which they interpret this process is very different. According to Dahrendorf, capitalism is merely an early form of industrial society, the type of society which is inevitably due to dominate our epoch. The disappearance of capitalism comes about through a relatively smooth process of social development, governed primarily by the economic changes involved in the spread of industrialisation. For Marx, on the other hand, the transcendence of capitalism could only be achieved as a process of revolutionary change, producing a very different type of society: socialism. Marx believed, moreover, that class conflict would play a fundamental role in this process of transition. Now Dahrendorf, in common with other theorists of industrial society, accepts that struggle between classes is a phenomenon of some significance in recent history. His views on this matter are complex, and I shall not attempt to summarise them here, since they involve certain proposals for reformulating the notion of 'class' that have not found much favour even among those otherwise close to his standpoint. So far as comparison with Marx is concerned, however, it is enough to say that Dahrendorf relegates class conflict in Marx's sense – as bound up with private property – to a relatively short period of time in the nineteenth century. Class conflict expresses major tensions to which the initial development of industrial society is subject, since its newly emerging institutions have not yet become fully formed. Dahrendorf accords particular importance here to the themes I have mentioned in points (3) and (4) above: the emergence of the liberal-democratic state; and the creation of forms of industrial arbitration, including legal recognition of the right to strike, whereby conflicts in the industrial sphere become regulated or controlled. The former makes possible the organisation of parties which can act to further divergent class interests in the political arena; the latter permits similar recognition of differences of interests in the industrial sector. The outcome is the 'de-fusing' of the ticking bomb of class conflict; the relatively violent class struggles of the nineteenth century cede place to peaceful political competition and industrial negotiation.

An industrial society, in Dahrendorf's analysis, is a differentiated society: one in which there is a multiplicity of cross-cutting conflicts and alliances. The general picture which he presents is an optimistic one. Such conflicts are well contained within the fabric of the institutional order of polity and economy as just described. A particularly important adjunct to this is the extension of equality of opportunity made possible by the growth of social mobility. As Dahrendorf portrays them, industrial societies are not egalitarian, in the sense that there remain substantial differences in wealth and power among different groupings within them. But the potentially disruptive effects of this are counterbalanced by the increasing possibilities open to individuals of movement up the social scale. Education plays a major role here. In an industrial society, according to Dahrendorf, success or otherwise in the educational system becomes the main influence affecting the location of individuals in society. The liberalising effects of the social mobility made possible through education are vital to the stable maturation of the industrial societies. In Dahrendorf's words, 'Social mobility has become one of the crucial elements of the structure of industrial societies, and one would be tempted to predict its "breakdown" if the process of mobility were ever seriously impeded' (Dahrendorf, p. 57).

Dahrendorf's ideas on this point come very close to those of Durkheim, written some half a century previously. Durkheim made a distinction between what he called 'internal' and 'external' inequalities. Internal inequalities are those which derive from genetic differences in capabilities or aptitudes; external inequalities are those which are social in origin. The general trend of development in contemporary societies, he proposed, is towards the progressive elimination of external inequalities. This does not imply a general egalitarianism in society as such, but increasing equality of opportunity through social mobility. Such a process can be interpreted as conforming more and more to a social order in which divisions of wealth or power are allocated solely according to internal inequalities. Individuals will find social positions commensurate with their talents, helped along by the guiding hand of a friendly state.

Marx: Capitalism and Socialism

As I have pointed out, Marx's writings have triggered a range of varying intellectual traditions, some of which occupy a central position in contemporary debates in the social sciences. For purposes of simplicity, I shall use as a basis for comparison with the theory of industrial society a work that has had just as strong an impact in sociology as has Dahrendorf's book. The views expressed therein, however, contrast considerably with those of the former author, since the work is a declaredly Marxist one: Ralph Miliband's *The State in Capitalist Society* (London, Weidenfeld & Nicolson, 1969). Miliband's objectives are much the same as those of Dahrendorf – to analyse the changes that have taken place in the industrialised countries over the past century and a half, and to consider the implications of Marx's writings for examining these changes. But while Dahrendorf argues that some of Marx's most basic ideas are thereby shown to be invalid, Miliband holds that they are essentially correct and have lost little of their explanatory power with the passing of time. Of course, Miliband accepts that the period since Marx's death has witnessed far-reaching social, economic, and political changes. But these can be understood by elaborating upon Marx's conceptions rather than by radically altering or abandoning them.

Miliband writes of 'capitalist society' rather than 'industrial society'. In so doing, he makes explicit his adoption of Marx's standpoint. Let me sketch in what this standpoint involves. Marx regarded capitalism as both a form of economic enterprise and, since he believed other institutions to be closely involved with this mode of economic organisation, a type of society. Fundamental to Marx's view is the presumption that the origins of capitalism, as a type of economic enterprise, were established well before the industrial revolution, and in fact provided the stimulus for the onset of industrialisation. Capitalistic economic enterprise, according to Marx, involves two essential structuring elements. One, of course, is capital. 'Capital' is simply any asset that can be invested so as to secure further assets: it thus includes money, the most fluid form of capital of all, and the means that make production possible: workshops, tools, and so on; and, after the phase of industrialisation, factories and machines.

The early accumulation of capital took place in the seventeenth and eighteenth centuries in Europe, and set under way massive processes of social and political transformation. The significance of such transformation, according to Marx, cannot be grasped without reference to the second element involved in the constitution of capitalistic enterprise. The accumulation of capital presupposes the formation of 'wage-labour', this referring to workers who, in Marx's phrase, have been 'expropriated from their means of production'. In feudal society, the mass of the population were peasants, achieving their livelihood from tilling small plots of land. As the development of capitalism accelerated, large numbers of peasants, through a mixture of inducement and coercion, moved from the land into the expanding urban areas. They formed a pool of labour, dependent upon the owners of capital for employment to sustain a livelihood. Capitalist economic organisation, for Marx, thus *presupposes* a class system based upon the relation between capital and wage-labour. The growth of machine production and the spread of the factory – in other words, the process of industrialisation – accelerated the transmutation of rural labourers into an urban-based, industrial working class.

According to Marx, capitalism is hence intrinsically a class society; and the class relations upon which it is founded are intrinsically ones of conflict or struggle. Employers and workers are in one important sense dependent upon one another. The former need a labour force that will engage in economic production; the latter, since they are propertyless, need the wages that employers pay them. But this dependence, according to Marx, is strongly imbalanced. Workers have little or no formal control over the work they do; employers are able to generate profits which they appropriate for their own purposes. The class relations of capitalism are exploitative, and promote chronic forms of conflict. Marx believed that class conflict, far from being confined to the early stages of capitalist development, would become progressively more acute over time.

In Marx's theory, class relationships directly link the economic organisation of capitalism to the institutions comprising the rest of the society. Not the examination of industrialisation as such, but the analysis of class structure, provides the chief basis of grasping the significance of the twin revolutions that have brought the modern world into being – and of indicating the future trajectory of its development. The increasing dominance of capitalistic production, which for Marx is a restlessly expanding system, propelled the technical innovations associated with the industrial revolution. The 1789 revolution in France, and other 'bourgeois' revolutions, according to Marx, signalled the rise to *political* power of the capitalist class. The emergence of democratic politics, involving parliamentary government, was for Marx closely tied to the economic changes which the spread of capitalist enterprise had brought about. In feudal society, feudal bondage or vassalage was the primary foundation of the class system; the mass of the population were expressly excluded from participation in government. In struggling to achieve political power, the capitalist class sought to destroy feudal privileges; participation in politics was in principle to be open to all, since everyone was henceforth regarded as an equal 'citizen' in the state.

In Marx's view, however, the capitalist state falls far short of achieving the democratic ideals which it supposedly exemplifies. The freedoms for which the rising entrepreneurial class and its allies fought in fact serve to support its domination over the working class. The state is not the beneficent liberal agency portrayed in the theory of industrial society, but an expression of class power. This is so in two senses, one more profound than the other. In the capitalist state, everyone is supposedly an equal citizen, with rights of political participation open to everyone alike. However, in most capitalist societies prior to the twentieth century, the majority of the population was effectively denied voting rights, because of property qualifications upon the right to vote; and the formation of labour parties was frequently frustrated, or directly prohibited by law. But these phenomena do not form the main basis of the class character of the capitalist state. For the sphere of the 'political' touches only a very restricted part of a person's life activity, not extending to that area in which much of day-to-day life is concentrated: work. In feudal society, the relations between lord and serf, or between master and journeyman, were ones having mutual rights and obligations, however much these were imbalanced in favour of one side rather than the other. A distinctive feature of the capitalist labour contract, by contrast, is that it is purely economic, a monetary relation. The worker is not accorded any rights of participation in the policies which govern the nature of the labour task or other aspects of the work setting. The formation of unions, one major aspect of class conflict according to Marx, represents an attempt of workers to gain a measure of control over the conditions of their labour.

These ideas form the backdrop to Miliband's analysis of the contemporary Western societies, and he challenges in a systematic way the picture portrayed by Dahrendorf. According to Miliband, private ownership of capital remains a key distinguishing feature of these societies, notwithstanding the growth of the large corporations and the increasing intrusion of the state into the economy. In Miliband's words:

[the capitalist societies] have in common two crucial characteristics: the first is that they are all highly industrialised societies; and the second is that the largest part of their means of economic activity is under private ownership and control. These combined characteristics are what makes them advanced capitalist countries in the first place and what distinguishes them radically from under-industrialised countries, such as India or Brazil or Nigeria, even though there too the means of economic activity are predominantly under private ownership and control; and from countries where state ownership prevails, even though some of them, like the Soviet Union, Czechoslovakia and the German Democratic Republic, are also highly industrialised. The criterion of distinction, in other words, is the level of economic activity combined with the mode of economic organisation. (Miliband, p. 9.)

The expanding importance of the large corporations, far from undermining capitalism, have consolidated the power of capital, albeit in a form which differs from ninenteenth-century entrepreneurial capitalism. Miliband denies that the separation of ownership from control has had anything like the radical consequences suggested by Dahrendorf. For one thing, the split has not progressed as far as is often claimed; minority stock ownership can still retain control of a corporation if the rest of its shares are dispersed. More importantly, capital-owners and managers have similar economic interests in sustaining the framework of capitalist production, tend to come from similar backgrounds of privilege, and hence constitute a relatively unified dominant class.

Social mobility is also much more limited than Dahrendorf avers, both in its extent and in its consequences for society at large. Most mobility, Miliband claims, is 'short-

range'. That is to say, it is between positions close to one
another in the class system; there is very little 'long-range'
mobility allowing those from working-class backgrounds to
move into elite groups. The equality of opportunity which
Dahrendorf regards as so important is more a myth than
a reality. Even if the facts of the matter had been as
Dahrendorf describes them, Miliband argues, mobility
would do little to alter class divisions. For the overall
class system would remain basically the same even if there
were a great deal more social mobility than there actually
is: 'Even a more "meritocratic" way to the top, grafted
to the existing economic system, would only ensure that
a larger number of people of working-class origin would
occupy the top rungs of the *existing* system. This may be
thought desirable, but it would not cause its transformation
into a *different* system' (Miliband, p. 41).

  Miliband's analysis of the consequences of the attainment of the universal franchise and of recognised procedures of arbitration in industry similarly contrasts with
that offered by Dahrendorf. The latter tends to present
these developments as the direct outcome of the pro-
gression of industrialisation, cohered and furthered by a
benevolent state. But for Miliband they have been
achieved *in and through* processes of class struggle, and
continue to be the focus of such struggle. The franchise
was rarely conceded easily by the dominant class; nor
were rights of industrial arbitration. Has the bomb been
successfully de-fused? Here, in spite of their divergent
starting-points, there is a certain measure of agreement
between Miliband and Dahrendorf. For Miliband accepts
that the scenario envisaged by Marx has not, thus far at
least, been realised. In Eastern Europe, there are societies
in which the official orthodoxy claims to embody Marx's
doctrines in practical form. Thus the Soviet Union, the
East European societies and China, as well as many other

countries in the world, are self-expressedly governed according to Marxist tenets.

As the paragraph quoted from Miliband above indicates, he recognises that these societies differ structurally from those of the West, since the economy is substantially controlled by the state rather than by private capital. But he does not accept that this has produced socialism such as Marx foresaw, only at best an incomplete and deformed version of it.

In the West, according to Miliband, while significant advances have been made over the harsh economic conditions of early capitalism, the challenge posed by the working class has been in some part blunted. On the economic level, class conflict is characteristically subject to strong pressures, exerted by business and by the state, to keep what has come to be called 'industrial relations' separate from political confrontations. The very success of unions in mobilising as 'organised labour' has tended to lead to their co-optation within the existing order. Unions which develop into large, bureaucratised organisations, having a full-time officialdom, can become detached from the membership they are supposed to represent on the shop-floor.

A variety of factors, Miliband adds, have contributed to parallel developments in politics. Since Marx's time, socialist or labour parties have come into positions of some power in all the advanced capitalist societies, with the notable and much-discussed exception of the United States – in which it can, however, be argued with some plausibility that the Democratic Party tends on the whole to represent the interests of labour. None of these parties has led a successful socialist revolution. Why not? One set of factors involved concerns the conditions under which socialist parties have managed to gain an effective foothold in government. Very often this has been achieved only where the parties concerned have entered into coalitions with their conservative rivals, in which the latter have held numerical supremacy; the result has then been to shore up the existing order rather than to undermine it. Where socialist parties have come into power as majorities, other factors have limited their impact. In order to achieve broad electoral success, they have generally had to dilute their programmes of social change. Once in power, their actual policies have been even less radical than their campaign promises, since strong resistance is put up by vested interests to threats to their established positions or privileges. Marxists have been divided about this, but Miliband inclines to the view that 'parliamentary socialism' is *ipso facto* likely to be ineffective; radical social change would need the additional support of extra-parliamentary movements.

Now there is no doubt that Marx believed socialist revolution in the developed capitalist countries to be imminent in the late nineteenth century. Something certainly has gone wrong. Miliband, however, looks to Marx's own writings for an answer. The reformist tendencies of Western socialist parties have been pervasively shaped by the influence of *ideology*. According to Marx, the class that controls the means of production and the political apparatus also controls the dominant symbols or forms of belief in a society. In capitalist societies, there is what Miliband calls an 'engineering of consent', whereby general attitudes of compliance to the status quo are fostered among the population. A range of institutions is involved in creating an ideological climate favourable to the continuation of capitalism, including especially educational institutions. Whereas Dahrendorf sees education as a prime vehicle of equalisation, and as promoting a fluid, 'meritocratic' social order, in Miliband's eyes education is a major phenomenon inhibiting social change.

For the educational system is geared to re-creating in each generation overall values that favour the interests of the dominant class.

The theory of industrial society, as I have mentioned previously, stands in blunt opposition to Marx's views in respect of the potentialities for radical transformation in the 'advanced societies'. The idea of the underlying unity of industrialism plays an important role in this standpoint. If industrial societies inevitably have common traits, possible models for the future are obviously fairly confined; the future, in other words, will not deviate much from the present. My arguments in the opening chapters of this book, I hope, will have already disposed the reader to be suspicious of any theory which is framed in terms of inevitabilities. This applies also to Marxist views that have been formulated in a similar way. There are Marxists who have argued that the dissolution of capitalism and its replacement by socialism is inevitable, and there are passages in Marx's writings where he also talks in such terms. Neither view is either logically defensible or empirically plausible. We confront a world of open possibilities, in which our knowledge of that world helps to shape what those possibilities are. But it is certainly important to assess which of the two perspectives just outlined is the more accurate, for this will strongly influence our notions of what trends of development are most likely in the world, and what the most realistic options are for influencing directions of social change.

3

Class Division and Social Transformation

The preceding chapter raises a cluster of different issues, some of which, although I hope they will prompt the reader's interest, I shall have no space to discuss in any detail in this book. There are three themes raised thus far upon which I want to focus particular attention, however. One is that of the significance of class analysis for the study of the industrially advanced societies today. Developments have not followed the lines Marx anticipated. But should we therefore declare his ideas to be no longer of any importance for analysing contemporary societies – as the theorists of industrial society are prone to claim? This question will be my main concern in the present chapter. The second theme concerns the nature of the state. According to the theory of industrial society, and according to liberal political theory more generally, the state is arbiter of the interests of the community in general. In Marx's view, by contrast, as Miliband makes clear, the state is a 'capitalist state': that is to say, the state is in some sense (which, as we will see, needs elucidation) an expression of class rule, reflecting an asymmetry of class interests. The problem of the state I shall take up in the next chapter. There is a third theme, however, that runs more deeply than these, and connects closely to the theoretical discussion in the opening chapters. This is the theme of the potentialities of social transformation in the world today. On one level this concerns the viability of the Marxian project. Can we still realistically envisage the possibility of the emergence of socialist societies that will differ radically from existing forms of industrial capitalism? On a more abstract, but no less significant, level, the third theme concerns the nature of sociology as a critical enterprise. I have claimed that social science stands in an inherently critical relation to its 'subject-matter' – the lives of human beings in society. But just what form should this critical enterprise take? In a sense, the whole book addresses this issue; but I shall confront it in an explicit way in the conclusion to the work.

Changes Since the Nineteenth Century: Corporate Power

If one compares the respective analyses offered by Dahrendorf and Miliband – symptomatic of many others on each side – there is not a great deal of divergence in their views about nineteenth-century Europe. To express the matter rather crudely, each agrees that Marx's portrayal of nineteenth-century industrial capitalism was essentially correct. Dahrendorf accepts that at that period private property and class division did coincide, and that open class struggle was a frequently observed phenomenon. The differences between the two authors are most clearly evident in respect of the changes which have occurred in the Western societies over the past one hundred years. For Dahrendorf, these changes are profound, and in an evolutionary rather than a revolutionary manner have dissolved the class character of capitalism such as Marx analysed it. Miliband rejects this interpretation. the Western societies remain capitalist societies, and class analysis is of primary importance in understanding their institutional form.

A comprehensive examination of a century of change would, of course, be well beyond the scope of this chapter – indeed beyond the scope of any single book. But it is possible to offer a broad appraisal, informed by empirical illustration, of the significance of the more far-reaching transmutations which have taken place. One evident feature of Western societies over the past hundred years is the increasing intrusion of the state into economic life, as well as into other spheres of social activity. But this is a phenomenon I shall consider more directly in the chapter which follows. More important at this juncture is the increased *concentration of the economy*: the domination of economic life by very large companies. No one disputes that, in all Western economies, in varying degrees, large corporations have come to occupy an increasingly prominent role. It is difficult to get precise figures, especially data that can be compared among countries. In the United States, the two hundred largest manufacturing firms have increased their share of total assets by 0.5 per cent each year since the turn of the century. These two hundred corporations today control some three-fifths of all manufacturing assets. Similarly, the two hundred largest financial organisations now are responsible for more than half of all financial transactions (Michael Useem, *The Inner Circle*, New York, Oxford University Press, 1984, chapter 2). The top handful of such companies are very large indeed, and have subsidiary companies all over the world.

The level of industrial concentration in Britain, as measured by most indices, is even higher than that of the United States. While the other Western European countries and Japan vary considerably in terms of concentration levels, in all of them large corporations play a major part in economic activity. The vast majority of very large companies are public corporations: that is to say, they float shares which can be bought and sold. The companies are 'owned' by their shareholders.

But what are the implications of all this? Dahrendorf follows those who have adopted what has generally come to be called a 'managerialist position'. The rise of the large corporations has entailed a fragmentation of the capitalist class such as it existed in the nineteenth century. The diversification of share-holding in the very large firms, according to this view, has several major consequences. Let me henceforth refer to such firms as the 'megacorporations'. The megacorporations, it is argued, are 'less capitalistic' than firms used to be in the heyday of entrepreneurial capitalism. Nineteenth-century capitalism was strongly competitive, and hence the main imperative of every company was the maximisation of profit. But the megacorporations now have such a commanding position in certain sectors of the economy that they are able to dominate markets, rather than being dominated by them. In addition, so the argument continues, they become more concerned with stable, long-term growth than with the immediate maximising of profits. Thus IBM is likely to place at least as much emphasis upon sustaining its overall development as upon the promotion of high levels of profit. In the jargon of modern economics, such firms tend to become 'satisficers'. What matters is that a satisfactory overall level of profitability is maintained, not that profits should be maximised above all else.

This interpretation meshes closely with the thesis that the formal owners of the megacorporations, the shareholders, no longer exert any significant control over corporate affairs. Power has passed to the managers. Since managers are not 'capitalists' – they do not own the corporations they control – they are more interested in the internal administrative stability of the firm than in the level of profit it achieves. Some managerialist writers have made a great deal of this. The megacorporation, they have asserted, has become a socially responsible agency, a 'soulful corporation' far removed from the aggressive, self-seeking entrepreneurial firm of the nineteenth century.

According to managerialist writers, such as Berle, the strongly marked concentration of corporate activity characteristic of contemporary Western economies does not imply the consolidation of a new form of upper class. Corporate concentration goes hand in hand with the dissolution of pre-existing forms of class solidarity. Drawing upon this literature, Dahrendorf speaks of the 'decomposition of the ruling class'. In the nineteenth century, there existed a unified capitalist dominant class, but the separation of ownership from control with the growth of the megacorporations has led to its disintegration. Capital 'owners' are a fragmented category, since share-holding has become fairly widespread among the population. The capital owners are separated from the managerial executives, who hold real power in the corporations. But the managers are also divided among themselves, since their main loyalties are to the particular corporations in their charge.

However, there are good reasons to object to each of the points involved in the above interpretation. The dominance of modern economies by the megacorporations has obviously had significant consequences for contemporary economic life. But these consequences do not seem to conform to the satisficing model proposed by managerialism. First of all, the managerialists tend to exaggerate the degree to which unfettered competition, geared to the maximisation of profits, was characteristic of nineteenth-century capitalism. Early entrepreneurs were often very much concerned with building up their companies in the long term, rather than simply with grabbing as much profit as possible. Perhaps more important, the megacorporations today still do operate in a competitive capitalistic framework, although there is no doubt that, through large-scale advertising and other means, they are able to influence demand in a direct fashion. The giant corporations are very rarely in a situation of 'monopoly' in a strict sense: that is, a circumstance where the firm is the sole producer of goods in a given sector of an economy. Usually the megacorporations are in competition with each other, both within the framework of national economies and especially, in the present era, on an international level. The pressures of such competition, and the drive to sustain high margins of profitability, may be very intense indeed. In parenthesis it should be noted that the managerialist approach was most popular in the 1950s and 1960s, when Western industry was in a phase of apparently steady, and relatively unproblematic, expansion. The resurgence of economic crisis in subsequent years, taken together with the rising importance of indigenous producers located in partially industrialised countries, having low labour costs, has today created major difficulties of profitability for the megacorporations in some economic sectors. Few can be satisfied to satisfice, if they ever were.

These considerations are germane to considering the nature and implications of the split between ownership and control. Recent evidence has placed in question both how far the managerialists are correct in maintaining that share-holding has become diversified in the megacorporations, and whether the diversification that has occurred has led to as dramatic a loss of control on the part of capital as has been presumed. Relatively small capital-holdings may be enough to secure effective control of corporate policy in any case, if the remainder of the stock ownership is fragmented. More important than these matters, however, is the fact that the interests of managers are much closer to those of owners than is postulated by the managerialist authors. Most top managers own considerable share-holdings, which are often very substantial in absolute terms, even if not large relative to the total wealth of a very large corporation. Their interests are thus 'capitalistic', in fact, in a double sense. They have a general interest in the prosperity of the stock-market, in common with other capital owners; and their activities within the sphere of the megacorporation are oriented within a framework of capitalistic enterprise. (For a discussion, see Edward S. Herman, *Corporate Control, Corporate Power*, Cambridge, Cambridge University Press, 1981.)

Such an analysis hardly lends support to the idea that a unified nineteenth-century capitalist class has ceded place to a diversified series of groups, to which the term 'dominant class' has no application. Of course, it is always possible to exaggerate the degree of unity of classes, both dominant and subordinate. We should not forget, for instance, that traditional land-owners still occupied leading positions of economic power in many Western societies in the nineteenth century. This certainly divided the upper class at least as much as whatever cleavages may today separate 'managers' from 'capitalists'. Two further factors are also relevant here. One is the continuing existence of pronounced inequalities in the distribution of wealth in the capitalist societies. Although there are certain variations among different countries, in all a small minority of the population owns a quite disproportionate amount of the total wealth. Minority ownership is even more pronounced if we consider stocks and shares specifically, rather than wealth in general. A second factor is social mobility – or rather the lack of it, so far as the composition of elite groups is concerned. Miliband's conclusions here seem closer to the mark than those of Dahrendorf. Whatever mobility may take place at lower levels of the class system, the chances of those from lowly backgrounds penetrating to the highest echelons are slim indeed.

The 'Institutionalisation of Class Conflict'

What, then, of the working class, whom Marx in a famous phrase referred to as the 'gravediggers of capitalism'? The grave remains undug, a century later; and its prospective incumbent, if no longer in the first flush of youth, does not seem seriously threatened by imminent demise. Why has the revolutionary transformation of capitalism not occurred? For writers of otherwise quite different persuasions, as we have seen, agree that there were at least substantial elements of validity in Marx's ideas in the nineteenth-century context. The answer to these questions – or the perspective which might be developed in respect of an answer – depends in some large degree upon interpreting the 'institutionalisation of class conflict'. I have put the phrase inside quote marks because I want to indicate that there is something suspect about it. But the processes to which it directs our attention are those whereby the working class has apparently become incorporated within the capitalist system, rather than posing a revolutionary alternative to it.

The phrase 'the institutionalisation of class conflict' is the preferred one of the theorists of industrial society, and serves to encompass rather neatly one of their distinctive emphases. For according to these writers, class struggle of an open or a disruptive kind is precisely confined to the early phases in the development of industrial capitalism. The development of accepted or regularised modes of industrial arbitration serves to blunt the edge of class conflict, transforming it into 'industrial conflict'. Workers are able to achieve a fair slice of the industrial cake because they have channels open to them for the pursuit of their economic interests. Access to rights of industrial bargaining have been complemented by the acquisition of political rights in the state. Those who have adopted this standpoint have pointed to the history of labour movements which, in the late nineteenth century or early twentieth centuries, had strong affiliations with Marxist doctrines, but which subsequently have abandoned a revolutionary posture in favour of reformism. The German and Swedish labour movements are often singled out as exemplary cases here. The German Social Democratic Party (SPD) in the latter part of the nineteenth century became the first mass political party specifically to embrace a Marxist stance. At the outset of the First World War, however, the majority of the members of the SPD voted to throw their weight behind the German war effort, eventually coming to assume the reins of government. They did so, however, as a party specifically concerned to crush the remains of the revolutionary left – those who had refused to fall into line with the majority of the party. This they accomplished bloodily, by the use of armed force; and in the intervening years the SPD has remained very much a party of social reform rather than one oriented to revolution. In the industrial sphere, meanwhile, German workers have been something of a model example of a compliant labour force, having one of the lowest strike rates in the industrialised world.

The development of the German labour movement,

however, can hardly be regarded as typical of that of Western societies as a whole; neither, more generally, can the pattern of change from a self-professedly revolutionary party to a reformist one. There are major, and long-entrenched, differences among the capitalist societies in these respects. On the one hand, there are those societies (such as the United States and Britain) in which revolutionary elements in the labour movement have been distinctly muted, and in which Marxism as a body of thought and a political programme has made little impact. On the other hand, there is no shortage of instances in which labour movements have had strong revolutionary traditions in the past, and which retain something of that character today. France and Italy fall into such a category. These differences show that the 'incorporation' of the working class is not a unitary phenomenon. If the maturation of capitalism does not bring about the rise of a revolutionary proletariat, neither is the working class everywhere docilely made 'part of the system'.

There seems little reason to doubt that the absence of revolutionary transformation in the West is closely bound up with the happenings pointed to by Dahrendorf and others. One of the best analyses of this, which Dahrendorf and writers having similar views have drawn upon extensively, is that of T. H. Marshall, written some thirty years ago (T. H. Marshall, 'Citizenship and social class', in *Class, Citizenship and Social Development*, Westport, Greenwood, 1973 [originally published 1950]). According to Marshall, the class conflicts characteristic of the nineteenth century have been progressively softened by the successive development of three types of 'citizenship rights'. These he refers to as civil, political, and social rights of citizenship. The first, civil citizenship, involves formal equality before the law, a cluster of rights of access to the legal system. The second refers above all to the universal franchise, and to the right to form political parties. The third refers to rights of industrial bargaining and of welfare – unemployment pay, sickness benefits, and so on. Marshall's idea is that each type of citizenship has been a platform for the development of the others. The legal rights which define every citizen as being 'free and equal' before the law were established in the relatively early phases of the formation of capitalism. Without these (which contrast with the differentiated rights and obligations of the Estates in feudalism), the extension of rights of political citizenship would have been impossible. The expansion of political rights in turn played a major part in limiting the power of the capitalist class, by allowing workers to organise politically to represent their interests in the parliamentary sphere. The increased political power of the working class, in conjunction with legal rights, helped to consolidate recognised modes of collective bargaining in industry. But the political rights of the working class, in Marshall's view, have been particularly important in fostering the modern 'welfare state'. Taken together, these developments have markedly altered both the impact of class divisions and the nature of class conflict. Over the past hundred years, Marshall says, 'citizenship and the capitalist class system have been at war' (Marshall, p. 84). Moreover, it is the former which is the victor, without its triumph being complete; for class struggle no longer threatens to topple the capitalist order.

I think there is a considerable amount of validity in what Marshall has to say, but it cannot be accepted just as it stands; there are several rather important qualifications to be made. The first concerns the significance of legal rights. Marshall does not sufficiently emphasise the imbalanced character of the relation between 'bourgeois legal relations' and the position of the wage-worker. As Marx went to some lengths to emphasise, the freeing of the mass of the population from ties of feudal obligation was part of their very subjection to the power of capital. Early capitalist entrepreneurs were interested in the creation of a pool of available 'free' labour that could be hired or fired at will. The *capitalist labour contract* has a focal part to play in Marx's analysis of capitalist economic enterprise, and connects through in a direct way to his theory of the state. The capitalist labour contract presupposes formally 'free' individuals, not bound to each other by feudal relations of fealty; the relation is a purely economic one, formed by a contract freely entered into. But this 'freedom' actually serves to enhance the power of employers over workers. For propertyless workers are necessarily dependent upon paid employment in order to survive. The legal rights that underlie freedom of contract do not permit the worker any degree of formal control over the process of labour in which he or she is involved. For Marx, as I have pointed out in the preceding chapter, this is a fundamental limitation to the system of parliamentary democracy. The political rights accorded to everyone as a citizen do not extend to the industrial sphere, the very area that occupies a large portion of the life-activity of the mass of the population.

This leads to a second observation. The expansion of citizenship rights which Marshall describes was not merely the result of the activities of a beneficent state, but (as Miliband notes) had to be actively fought for. It is worthwhile at this point repeating the emphases I made in the opening sections of this book. It is not 'citizenship and the class system' as such which have been at war with one another; rather, each expresses the active engagements of human agents in the institutional context of early capitalist development. Marx's standpoint –

appropriately elaborated upon – still provides a basis for analysing such processes and their outcome. The intersection among legal, political, and welfare rights provides a focus for continuing class conflict; these are not just successive phases in the amelioration of class inequalities, but remain today at the centre of continuing conflicts. The expansion of citizenship rights is in substantial degree the achievement of labour movements, entering into conflict with employers and with the state. We can reinterpret Marshall's account in the following way. The growth of unionism among workers can be understood as a 'defensive' response to the lack of power on the part of the working class, built into the capitalist labour contract. Having no formal rights of participation in the sphere of production, workers have adopted various modes of withdrawal of co-operation – based on the threat or actuality of the collective withdrawal of labour – in order to achieve some degree of control over the work setting. In many countries, as Miliband says, the establishment of recognised modes of industrial bargaining was accomplished only after a great deal of active, often bitter and violent, struggle on the part of labour movements. Much the same applies to the achievement of political rights. The universal franchise was in most countries only obtained in the twentieth century – under the impending shadow of war, reluctantly acceded to by governments wanting to mobilise their populations for hostilities.

What Marshall calls 'the welfare state' (of which more in the following chapter) Dahrendorf talks of as a 'post-capitalist' industrial order. The view I am suggesting is rather different. The Western societies have certainly changed significantly since Marx's day – such change being in some substantial part the very result of class conflict – but they remain 'capitalist'. The Western societies are capitalist societies in respect of the following criteria: (1) production for profit, involving the dominance of privately owned capital, remains the main dynamic impetus of the economic system; (2) ownership of private property, particularly capital ownership, remains highly unequal; (3) class conflict continues to be of primary significance in both the economy and polity. The capitalist societies are *class societies*.

This means that Marx's writings retain a core of relevance to analysing those societies. It does not, of course, imply that either Marx's own work, or that of subsequent Marxists, can be accepted uncritically. The contrasts I drew between the theory of industrial society and Marxism are a useful short-hand way of encompassing some of the main substantive problems of contemporary sociology. But I shall want to argue subsequently that we need in some part to break free from each of these competing styles of analysis.

New Classes, New Technologies

One of the most characteristic, and most discussed, changes that have taken place in the class systems of the Western societies in the past century is the relative growth of 'non-manual', or 'white-collar', work, compared with 'manual', or 'blue-collar', labour. According to census statistics, there is now a higher proportion of white-collar workers than blue-collar workers in the labour force in the United States. In other countries the relative proportion of white-collar workers, as indicated by governmental statistics, is not as high, but has followed a similar trend.

These statistics seem to run completely counter to Marx's portrayal of the probable development of the capitalist societies. For Marx appeared to believe that the vast majority of the population were destined to become manual workers in routinised occupations; small capital would largely evaporate, and a tiny class of large capitalists would confront a massive proletariat. There are some passages in Marx which go against such a simple view. The most famous of these is one in which Marx speaks of 'the constantly growing number of the middle classes, those who stand between the workman on the one hand and the capitalist and landlord on the other' (Karl Marx, *Theories of Surplus Value*, London, Lawrence & Wishart, 1969, vol. 2, p. 573). But the comment is made in a polemical context, and its implications are not elucidated. Many non-Marxists have in fact taken the spread of white-collar work to be a major element confuting Marx's analysis of the class structure of capitalism. Research studies in different countries mostly indicate that white-collar workers, or what has come to be called the 'new middle class', tend to have lower rates of unionisation than those in manual occupations, and also to have divergent values and attitudes. For some authors the relative growth of white-collar work thus signals the arrival of a 'middle-class society'. Marx had envisaged a society increasingly split between two contending classes. Instead, the expansion of the new middle class becomes a stabilising factor, eroding the working class; the proletariat is increasingly absorbed into the middle class, rather than vice versa.

Marxists have criticised this view in a convincing way. Two factors suggest caution in taking the statistics quoted above, which are official census figures, at their face value. One is that many white-collar occupations are of a routine, even mechanised, character; the growth in non-manual work has gone along with the 'mechanisation of the office'. Hence a considerable proportion of jobs that are categorised by the census as 'white-collar' are difficult to distinguish from manual occupations, and require little in the way of specific skills other than a general literacy. To be a 'clerk' in the nineteenth century was to be a professional worker, in a position of administrative authority. There are vastly more 'clerical' workers in the occupational system today; but clerical work has become reduced to a stereotyped and undemanding series of tasks that carry no prerogatives of authority at all. Second, the expansion of clerical labour has coincided with the increasing entry of women into the lower levels of the non-manual labour force. In most Western countries, women constitute the majority of those in clerical occupations (as well as those in a range of 'service occupations', such as shop assistants). The non-manual jobs in which women are clustered tend to be quite distinct from those staffed by male workers. These are the jobs that have become most routinised, in which job security is low and prospects of career advancement poor. Such women workers do not form part of a burgeoning and affluent new middle class; on the contrary, they are what I have called an 'underclass' of the white-collar sector (Anthony Giddens, *The Class Structure of the Advanced Societies*, London, Hutchinson, 1979, p. 288). Women are subject to double exploitation (see Chapter 6, below): discriminated against in the occupational system, they also characteristically have to bear the brunt of domestic work and child care in the home.

Some writers have gone on to argue that Marx's prognosis of the increasing 'proletarianisation' of the labour force is thereby vindicated. But there are relatively few who take such a view nowadays. Most recognise that, although the new middle class is not as large as is implied by those who adopt a naïve interpretation of census statistics, it is none the less a complicating element in capitalist class relations. White-collar workers in professional, managerial, or other administrative occupations have shown that they are capable of becoming a significant political force within the contemporary societies. Marx was right, broadly speaking, to anticipate the decline of owners of small capital – small businessmen, shopkeepers, and so on, the 'old middle class'. But to give sufficient weight to the influence of the propertyless new middle class means departing in some degree from Marx's formulations. This is my opinion, at any rate. To be fair, it should be pointed out that some recent Marxist writers have attempted to formulate analyses of the new middle class which they hold to be more directly derived from Marx than I think possible (see, for instance, E. O. Wright, *Class, Crisis and the State*, London, New Left Books, 1978, ch. 3).

New classes, new technologies. There are a number of influential authors, some close to a Marxist standpoint, the majority very distant, who have placed prime emphasis upon specific kinds of technological change as especially important in shaping the current trajectories of the capitalist societies. The most prominent conception here is that we are moving into an era which will no longer be dominated by manufacturing industry, as in the past, but instead by 'information technology'. These writers speak, not just of a 'post-capitalist society', but of a 'post-industrial' one. (For two contrasting versions of this idea see Daniel Bell, *The Coming of Post-Industrial Society*, New York, Basic Books, 1973; Alain Touraine, *The Post-Industrial Society*, New York, Random House, 1971.) The part played by science in modern production, the widespread adoption of computers and, most recently, of microchip technology, they claim, will have very profound consequences for the pre-existing social order.

Such consequences are indeed likely, although the introduction of microchip technology is so recent that its results are as yet rather imponderable. Certainly talk of a 'second industrial revolution' is, to say the least, premature. Moreover, there are strong objections which can be brought against the idea that industrialism is in the process of being superseded by a new *type of society*, that is, a 'post-industrial' order which will look distinctly different from the contemporary societies. Some of the most telling criticisms are these: (1) The notion of a post-industrial society continues the technological determinism that lurks not far from the surface of the theory of industrial society. As I have already stressed, we should beware of all types of determinism when applied to human affairs. No technology can be adequately studied in isolation from the social frameworks within which it is implicated. In the Western societies, these frameworks remain pre-eminently capitalistic in character. (2) Some authors have suggested that the imminent arrival of a post-industrial society signals the arrival of a new ruling class, whose power will be based upon control of information rather than of property. This notion is not actually in essence a new one, however, and dates as far back as the early nineteenth century. Saint-Simon's emergent 'industrial society', for example, was to be ruled by a combination of scientists and technical experts. It did not happen then, and notwithstanding the contemporary advances of information technology, it is not likely to happen now. (3) The social and economic changes linked to new technologies have to be understood – as the next chapter and subsequent chapters will help to make clear – in a world context. A good deal of manufacturing industry which supplies the West with a substantial proportion of its goods is now located outside of those societies themselves.

Japan was first of all the leader in this regard, moving in some three decades from a relatively lowly economic ranking to become the nation with the third highest GNP in the world (behind the United States and the USSR). Japan currently exports far more goods than it imports, and has both an investment rate and a growth rate twice that of the United States. It has come to assume a leading position in a succession of industries previously dominated by Western countries.

The Japanese have successfully challenged the sway the United States used to hold in 'basic' industries such as steel production and shipbuilding. Japan has wrested world leadership away from the United States and Germany in automobile production; from the UK and Holland in production of consumer electronics; from Germany and Switzerland in the production of cameras, watches and optical goods (Ezra F. Vogel, *Japan as Number One: Lessons for America*, Cambridge, Mass., Harvard University Press, 1979). But the position of Japan has in turn been put in question by the rapid economic development of other Eastern countries, in particular Hong Kong, Taiwan and South Korea.

As will be mentioned in a later chapter (pp. 146–52), these shifts have gone little way towards redressing the major imbalances that exist between the more privileged and the less privileged sectors of the world. But they have served to integrate Western countries within a progressively more complex international division of labour. The supposed coming of the post-industrial society is probably better described as a realignment of the world economy, in which the capitalist countries provide the administrative 'centre' of a world economic system (albeit one that may be undergoing significant processes of transition).

The End of the Working Class?

These things having been said, we certainly have to take seriously the idea that major transmutations are taking place in the class structure and in the nature of work in Western societies. It might be the case that the increasing

FIGURE 3.1   *Unemployment in a range of countries, 1973–83 (expressed as a percentage of the active labour force)*

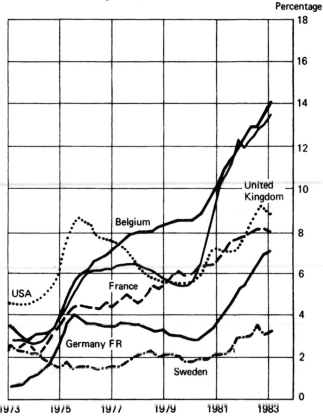

Source: *Social Trends*, London, HMSO, 1985.

use of information technology will progressively alter the character of the work many people do, and contribute to spreading unemployment. However, much of the world economy is, in addition, in the grip of a protracted recession, and rates of unemployment have risen sharply over recent years in many countries. In the light of these phenomena many have argued that the industrialised countries will never again return to a 'full employment' economy such as most enjoyed in the 1960s. Figure 3.1 gives an indication of changing levels of unemployment in a range of Western societies.

A variety of more or less speculative interpretations of trends of development in the class structure of Western countries has been put forward in the light of the possible persistence of high rates of unemployment. One of the more notable and provocative is that of the contemporary French writer, Gorz (André Gorz, *Farewell to the Working Class*, London, Pluto, 1982). Although he writes as a radical rather than a conservative, Gorz argues that the project of the revolutionary transformation of capitalism, such as Marx conceived it in the nineteenth century, is now dead. Rather than the proletariat over-throwing the capitalist system, the maturation of capital-ism serves increasingly to diminish the role of the working class. Gorz accepts the thesis that the ratio of blue-collar to white-collar work is steadily diminishing. But he adds to this the impact of information technology, which he believes will eradicate a large proportion of existing manual occupations – and the more routine white-collar ones too.

Gorz's critique of Marxism thus differs very consider-ably from the type of viewpoint represented by Dahren-dorf. In Marx's view, as Gorz portrays it at any rate, the potential of the working class to bring about a just and humane society is founded on the surplus production which industrial capitalism makes possible. Modern industries generate productive capabilities which create far more wealth than is necessary to meet basic human needs. In surplus production we see foreshadowed an area of freedom from the constraints of enforced labour; work will become an end in itself, governed only by the fulfilment which it offers to the producer. However, Gorz says, the subsequent evolution of capitalism has completely confounded these expectations. The adoption of strict work control practices by management has effectively squashed any consciousness workers might have had of the creative potential of labour. Many factories are today linked with production processes that may span several continents (see pp. 148–50), and they have long since ceased to be the main centres of the formulation of policy and the enactment of decisions. In an era of technically complex and global production processes, the only power that workers can possess in localised production settings is negative power – the capability in some degree to block management policies or initiatives.

But the very trends that have served to undermine the Marxian view, according to Gorz, create new possibilities for realising some of the values compatible with it. 'The point now', he argues, 'is to free oneself *from* work by rejecting its nature, content, necessity and modalities' (Gorz, p. 67). The issue is no longer, as Marx anticipated, the achievement of power by the working class, but attaining the freedom to reject the role of 'worker' altogether. The developments outlined above have replaced the working class with what Gorz calls a 'non-class of non-workers' or 'neoproletariat'. This is made up of large numbers of people who either are permanently unemployed, or if they are in work are in jobs that are poorly organised, lack a definite class identity and are low in job security. In the longer term, as a consequence of an expanding influence of information technology, the ranks of the unemployed will become further swelled.

Since it is not a class, and has no organisational coherence, the neoproletariat is not a substitute in current times for the working class in Marxist theory; it does not have an historical mission to change the social order. But this apparent weakness, Gorz proposes, is a source of strength. For those in the 'non-class' have no reason to accept the 'productionist' ethos of either capitalism, or of socialism as Marx envisaged it. They are more and more likely to seek sources of satisfaction which have nothing to do with work and the workplace. Diversity of lifestyles – external to the sphere of work – will become the keynote of the future. We are moving, Gorz claims, towards a 'dual society'. In one sector, production and political administration will be organised to maximise efficiency. The other sector will be a sphere in which individuals occupy themselves with the manifold pursuits to which the pursuit of enjoyment or self-fulfilment leads them.

So far as those in work are concerned, Gorz says, we can expect a major shortening of the average working day, and the extensive introduction of forms of job-sharing. Unemployment is seen by most employers and workers alike as a negative phenomenon; but this view is likely to become archaic. The productionist work ethic is giving way to a new outlook concerning the use of 'free-time', which will no longer be regarded as merely marginal to the day's activities. It is already the case in several European countries that a substantial proportion of employees choose not only the hours at which they begin and stop work, but, within limits, the amount of time they work per month. A range of other possibilities has been envisaged: 'retirement advances' given at any age, in return for a postponement of final retirement from the labour force; sabbatical leaves, such as are at present found only in a few settings, most notably universities; and 'time savings accounts' whereby individuals who have 'accumulated' a certain amount of work over a given period will be able to reduce the hours they work subsequently, without loss of earnings.

It is instructive to compare Gorz's views with those suggested by other authors, such as Himmelstrand and his colleagues (Ulf Himmelstrand *et al.*, *Beyond Welfare Capitalism*, London, Heinemann, 1981). Himmelstrand writes against the backdrop of Sweden – incidentally, the society which has probably made more extensive use of information technology than any other to date. Himmelstrand's work endorses just those phenomena Gorz declares obsolete; he offers a self-declaredly Marxist interpretation of the possibility of a process of socialist transformation led by the labour movement. Himmelstrand not only is reluctant to bid farewell to the working class, he denies both that it has shrunk in relative size and that workers are today passively incorporated into the technical apparatus of production. Sweden is one of the most materially prosperous, egalitarian and technologically advanced societies in the world – enjoying a per capita income superior to that of the United States. It is also one which has experienced not far off half-a-century of government by a professedly labour party, the Social Democratic Party. Just these facts, according to Himmelstrand, make it possible for Sweden to develop 'beyond welfare capitalism' towards socialism. As Himmelstrand understands it, 'socialism' here does not refer to anything like the East European model – which, in common with the majority of Western Marxists today, he disparages. What he wishes to see come about is not an extension of the nationalisation of industry or of centrally planned production. Rather, he sees the possibility of giving workers a measure of real control over the processes of production in which they are involved – something that Gorz dismisses as impossible to achieve in modern industry. In Himmelstrand's view, moreover, this is not just a prospect which someone with an eye to the future might see as desirable; it is on the agenda now.

In Sweden the unemployment level is low compared with most other Western countries. There is no talk in Himmelstrand's book of an increasingly populous neoproletariat of the unemployed or partly employed. He writes instead of what he calls the 'extended working class' – the majority of the labour force – who are presumed to hold overall interests in common in socialist reforms. The extended working class comprises all those having routine jobs, including lower-white-collar and service workers as well as the blue-collar working class. He tries to show that according to various indices of class consciousness the proletariat in the shape of the extended working class is not only alive but kicking. Conditions exist in Sweden and probably also in various of the other industrially advanced societies, for the development of programmes that will go beyond the usual trade-union negotiations towards a more far-reaching form of social reconstruction. More specifically, Himmelstrand draws attention to the proposals for introducing a system of wage-earners' funds into industry – proposals now officially sanctioned by the Social Democrats. Although various versions of these have been suggested, basically they involve profit-sharing. A certain proportion of company profits would be transferred to employees of firms each year, and also into national and regional development funds. This process could supposedly both progressively effect a shift in the power relation between employers and workers, and also be integrated with schemes of industrial democracy.

How is it possible that there could be such large differences of viewpoint between two authors, each writing about current developments in the class structure of Western societies? One answer, obviously, is that Himmelstrand's discussion is centred upon Sweden, even if its implications are not supposed to be limited to that society, whereas Gorz's primary point of reference is France. But there are also substantial discrepancies in what each writer believes the consequences of current changes in industrial organisation and class structure to be. One issue certainly concerns whether the working class is disappearing (as Gorz says) or expanding (as Himmelstrand claims) within the occupational system of Western societies.

The discussion I offered previously (pp. 56–61) is relevant to this question. It seems probable that neither author's views are correct. On the one hand, several of the major Western societies, including the United States, the United Kingdom, France and Germany, are experiencing a contraction of the 'older' industries such as coal-mining or iron and steel production. Some such production, as has been mentioned, has been appropriated by other countries in the Far East. On the other hand, the diminishing relative size of these industries has been complemented by the growth of service industries to do with, for example, hotels, restaurants and travel. The majority of jobs in these newer industries are unskilled or semi-skilled and, as I have pointed out earlier, cannot be regarded as propelling their incumbents into the 'middle class'. But neither do these categories of individuals tend to merge with blue-collar workers to form what Himmelstrand labels an 'extended working class'. The picture seems more one of diversification – with significant variations between as well as within the class structure of different societies.

Gorz's view depends not only upon the diminishing importance of the blue-collar working class, but also upon the claimed link between information technology and unemployment, together with the assumption that high levels of unemployment are here to stay for the indefinite future. But these claims are each debatable. It is clear enough that microelectronic technology, especially when involved in the automation of processes previously involving human labour, may make for redundancies in the immediate contexts in which it is introduced. But how far it does so, and will continue so to do, in relation to the economy as a whole remains a highly controversial matter. Some, like Gorz, hold that automation leads to a reduction in employment opportunities. But the argument can be made that the spread of information technology will in the shorter or longer run create new jobs, as patterns of demand shift. It is just as easy to think of ways in which the extended use of microtechnology might generate new employment as the reverse. Cheaper mass production of existing products might create new demand; new products might be initiated or novel services opened up; sectors of industry in financial difficulty might regain profitability.

All this therefore necessarily remains more problematic and unpredictable than many writers are prepared to admit. The high levels of unemployment of the present time have to be seen against the backdrop of the 1973–4 'oil crisis' and other factors tending to produce recession. It is certainly more than within the bounds of possibility that rates of unemployment will remain high, or increase further, in the majority of Western societies in the foreseeable future. But this is surely not as inevitable as many observers now assume. In the 1960s, the period of rising prosperity in all Western countries, it was taken for granted by almost everyone that something close to full employment was here to stay. We should be cautious of using the same type of over-generalised reasoning in reverse now.

These remarks have a bearing on the empirical basis of the views advanced respectively by Gorz and Himmel-strand. They plainly do not settle the issue of how relevant a scenario close to that envisaged by Marx more than a century ago still has relevance to defensible political programmes today. The problems involved here stretch well beyond the issues that have been analysed in this book thus far, and I shall return to them in the concluding chapter.

4

The Modern State

There is one highly important set of changes occurring over the past century to which I have so far referred only in passing: the expanding role of the state in social life. The enlargement of the activities of the state can be documented in various ways. On the economic level, the state in the capitalist societies has come to play an increasingly direct role in supervising productive activity. In most such countries the state directly employs over 40 per cent of the economically active labour force, who work either within its own administrative apparatus or in nationalised industries. States have also attempted more and more to 'intervene' in economic activity by seeking to influence the supply of and demand for goods, engaging in economic planning, prices and incomes policies, and so on. But the state also intrudes into a variety of other aspects of social life: participating in the foundation and organisation of prisons, asylums, hospitals, and in the provision of that array of services included under the general rubric of 'welfare'.

In view of this it is surprising that, at least until fairly recently, the state has been largely ignored in sociology – by those of a Marxist persuasion as well as by others. In part this circumstance arose as a consequence of an especially unfortunate division of labour in the social sciences. The objective of sociology, it was assumed, is the study of 'society', understood as what nineteenth-century thinkers used to call 'civil society': the economy, family, and other institutions outside the state. Analysis of the state was then allocated as the specific province of the discipline of 'politics', or 'political science'. In some degree, however, avoidance of study of the state has deeper intellectual roots, stretching back to the nineteenth century. Marxism and non-Marxist sociology have a common ancestry in the critique of classical economic theory. In the latter, the state was assigned a minimal role. According to the early economists, the most important driving forces of social change are centred in production, and therefore in the realm of 'civil society'. The state provides a legal framework which guarantees that economic contracts are protected, and generally oversees the interests of the community.

Later thinkers became dissatisfied with this view. For those standing in the mainstream of sociology – we might again instance Durkheim – the state has a more positive and significant part to play than the early economists suggested. The expansion of the activities of the state is a necessary and unobjectionable element in the development of a social order committed to progressive social reform. The state is seen here as a benign set of institutions that has a direct involvement in furthering the eradication of class divisions and inequalities. Marx's view, by contrast, was that the economists failed to recognise the class character of the state. Far from being a means of dissolving class divisions, the state is inherently involved with sustaining them: with protecting the interests of the dominant class against those of other classes in society. But in neither tradition of thought did the state become the object of systematic study. For non-Marxist and Marxist writers alike, the supposed *effects* of state activities were the focus of attention, rather than the state itself. Marx himself in fact left only a few fragmentary texts dealing with the state, his energies being concentrated upon criticising early economic theory on its own terrain: the relationships involved in capitalist production.

The State and Classes: Recent Views

Over the past decade or so, however, the modern state has become the subject of lively discussion, especially among Marxist authors. Marxists have become pointedly aware of the rudimentary character of accounts of the state contained in Marx's writings, and have sought to elaborate in some considerable detail upon their implications. Miliband's book, in fact, was one of the first contributions to this resurgent concern with the state. Two other influential authors in this field are Poulantzas and Offe. (See especially Nicos Poulantzas, *Political Power and Social Classes*, London, New Left Books, 1973 [first published 1968]; Claus Offe, *Disorganised Capitalism*, Cambridge, Polity Press, 1985). Miliband and Poulantzas have been involved in a series of direct interchanges about how the state should be analysed; these I remark upon briefly below.

The various comments that Marx made about the capitalist state can be construed in two ways. In some places Marx speaks as if the state were the direct instrument of class rule, controlled in an immediate way by the capitalist class. There is a passage, for example, where Marx talks of the state as the 'executive committee of the bourgeoisie'. But there are other contexts in which Marx seems to claim that the class character of the state consists in the fact that the state officialdom protects the overall continuity of capitalist production. Although it may not be obvious at first sight, there is potentially a very substantial difference between these two views. The first implies both that the dominant class is a unitary social formation, and that this class manipulates the state at will. Consequently, this standpoint is easily attacked, and it is this type of conception which has been challenged by so-called 'pluralist' writers. According to the pluralist interpretation, which fits closely with the ideas expressed by Dahrendorf and other advocates of the theory of industrial society, there is no homogeneous 'ruling class' in the Western societies. Instead, there exist diversified sets or pluralities of elites, each having only quite limited power to influence governmental policies.

The second view derived from Marx allows for the recognition that there may be considerable divisions, and frictions, within ruling circles, in a society which remains a class society. Poulantzas develops this standpoint in his writings on the state – albeit in an often ponderously obscure style, and in a way that is open to criticism. In the first interpretation of Marx mentioned above, the state appears as manipulated by the ruling class. According to Poulantzas, however, the state has what he calls a 'relative autonomy' from the capitalist class, which itself is characteristically internally divided. The state, in other words, has a certain degree of independent power, but no more than a certain degree; and this power is used to sustain the general institutional framework of capitalist enterprise. The state may initiate policies counter to the short-term interests of certain capitalistic groupings, in order to defend the longer-term interest of perpetuating the system as a whole. An example might be where the government introduces anti-trust legislation in the face of opposition from business leaders who wish to carry through a merger of firms in a particular economic sector.

This sort of analysis of the state is undeniably more

sophisticated than those based upon the first, or 'instrumentalist', interpretation of Marx. Poulantzas, in fact, regards Miliband's book as falling into this category, and on this basis has subjected it to critical attack. Miliband, Poulantzas argues, is too concerned to demonstrate that elites in the capitalist societies are cohered by common educational backgrounds, familial relationships, friendship relations, and so on. Miliband confronts the theory of industrial society, and political pluralism, too much in their own terms – trying to show that there does, after all, remain a coherent propertied class at the reins of government. But the existence of schisms in the upper echelons, Poulantzas argues, does not in and of itself show that capitalist class domination has been undermined. Such schisms are normal anyway. What is of decisive importance is that the institutional mechanisms of capitalist production persist.

Although the debate between Poulantzas and Miliband cannot be said to have been a particularly instructive or fruitful one – the participants too often talk past one another – it does highlight very well some of the general issues with which I introduced this book. For Poulantzas's overall standpoint, although a Marxist one, conforms closely to certain of the elements of the model of sociology which I criticised. In Poulantzas's scheme, which is strongly influenced by the 'structuralist Marxism' of the contemporary French philosopher Louis Althusser, social actors are explicitly regarded as 'bearers of modes of production'. Put in other terms, human agency is explained as the outcome of social causes. Human beings do not appear here as knowledgeable agents: their 'double involvement' with society is not conceptualised. Thus Miliband aptly criticises Poulantzas for indulging in what hc calls a sort of 'structural super-dctcrminism', whatever the rights and wrongs of the rest of the dispute (Ralph

Miliband, 'The capitalist state: a reply to Nicos Poulant-zas', *New Left Review*, no. 59, 1970).

Let me go a bit further with this point, for as well as reinforcing the importance of the theoretical consider-ations discussed in the opening chapter, it is directly germane to the question of the state. How does the state achieve this 'relative autonomy' that Poulantzas talks about; of what does it consist? Poulantzas's answers to these questions are vague and elusive. It is not clear what the relative autonomy of the state is based on, how relative it is, or what it is relative to. We can, I think, clarify these things, but only by departing from the sort of deterministic standpoint adopted by Poulantzas. The best way of clarifying some of the specific features of the capitalist state is by drawing a comparison with other types of states that have existed in history – agrarian states or empires. In most of the latter, the personnel of the ruling class were also the state officialdom; state and dominant class were one and the same. But in capitalist societies such is not the case. The members of the dominant class – that is, the leaders of business or industry – may quite often take a direct part in govern-ment. But by and large the industrial leadership and state officialdom are institutionally distinct from one another. In capitalism, to use the oft-quoted phrase of an early Marxist of the turn of the century, Karl Kautsky, 'the ruling class does not rule'. Both versions of what Marx had to say on the state in a sense agree on this, but its implications can be drawn in a way so as to illuminate the idea of relative autonomy.

The state in capitalism is dependent for its revenue upon the successful prosecution of business activity; it could not survive were it not for the prosperity of industrial enterprise, which, however, it does not directly control, such control being the province of the capitalist class. Autonomy of action on the part of state officialdom is thus strongly limited by its dependence upon capitalistic enterprise. This is the institutional setting for state autonomy, and at the same time the basic source of the limited or 'relative' nature of that autonomy. However, none of these phenomena can be, or should be, interpreted in a mechanical fashion. The increasing intrusion of the state into economic life is part and parcel of attempts of state personnel to influence the general operation of economic enterprise. It is not only Marxists who have been aware of the dislocations and crises to which capitalist economies tend to be subject. State administrators are as aware of this as anyone, and are chronically involved in seeking to 'manage' the economy.

So far, this is in general agreement with Poulantzas's views, although expressed in different terms from those he favours. But there is, I think, a further element of considerable importance relevant to the autonomy of the state. This is the power of the organised working class itself – expressed both as union power and in the influence of labour or socialist parties upon the conduct of government. Poulantzas explains why state and capitalist class should often be at odds solely in terms of divisions within that class: state politics may favour one sector of capital rather than another. But the state also has to attempt to cope with the influence of organised labour. If in the early years of industrial capitalism this was not of great moment, such is hardly the case today. The struggles and changes I have described in the preceding chapter have not just 'incorporated' the working class into economic and political institutions that have remained unaltered; the citizenship rights which have been won have shifted the balance of power in the state, even if they have not led to the revolutionary upheavals Marx foresaw.

Offe's writings at this point serve as an apt corrective to Poulantzas's emphases. According to Offe, the state cannot be adequately understood in terms of either version of Marx mentioned above, although the second is more nearly correct than the first. The state is actually sandwiched between two inherently antagonistic or 'contradictory' influences. The modern state is committed to a range of measures – including social welfare, but also a range of other services – provided for the community as a whole. But however much the state may attempt to 'manage' economic growth, its income is essentially dependent upon wealth generated by privately owned capital and the corporations: that is, upon processes which it does not directly administer. The services the state must organise have to be paid for by income derived indirectly, via taxation. But those who have command over economic life – the business leaders, or capitalist class – tend to resist the endeavours of the state to secure the income needed to provide these community services. This is because while some such services (e.g. the provision and maintenance of a good road system) are desired as much by the dominant class as by others, many (e.g. the provision of welfare benefits) are primarily utilised by those in the lower orders of society.

The result, according to Offe, is a constant tension between what he calls the 'commodification' and 'de-commodification' of social relationships. A commodity is any product or service that can be bought or sold; hence a commodified relationship is one that a price can be put on, that is marketable. De-commodification means removing social relationships from the marketplace, organising them by criteria other than the economic. Labour or socialist parties on the whole tend to create or pursue policies that expand non commodified relation ships. The promotion of educational opportunities or free hospital care for everyone would be examples. Conservative parties, on the other hand, drawing most of their support from the upper or middle classes, are likely to seek to preserve commodified relations, or even to 're-commodify' them. Such would be the case, for example, with governmental policies aimed at paying for the costs of education through loan schemes, or which extend the sphere of private medicine.

The sort of standpoint set out by Offe conforms in a general way to the discussion of the significance of citizenship rights and the nature of the 'welfare state' which I sketched in the preceding chapter. The theorists of industrial society have been inclined to treat these as 'completed' phenomena that have served to undergird a stable liberal-democratic industrial order; and they have seen them as having effectively dissolved class conflict in any sense close to that analysed by Marx. But if I am right, they are chronically enmeshed in class conflict rather than undermining it; and the 'welfare state' is thus a relatively fragile creation. In a political climate of conservatism such as today, this is easier to see than it was a decade or two ago, for some current conservative governments have mounted a more sustained attempt to 're-commodify' areas of welfare services than has been seen for a long time.

The State and Bureaucracy

If Marxist authors have contributed very substantially to the analysis of the modern state in the respects thus mentioned, there are two contexts in which their discussions have tended to be notably deficient. One is the association of the state with bureaucracy, and more generally with administrative power; the other is the association of the state with the *nation*, and of the *nation-state* with military power and *violence*. We cannot look to the theory of industrial society to provide a guide for coping with these issues either, because it is too much entangled with the traditions of thought from which Marxism derives.

There is, however, one major figure in social theory whose ideas do offer a resource for approaching such issues: Max Weber. Prior to Weber, the term 'bureaucracy' was generally used as equivalent to 'state bureaucracy', that is, as referring to state functionaries. Weber's writings on bureaucracy continue to be particularly concerned with the state, but he extends the term considerably, so that it has reference to any form of large-scale organisation. According to Weber, the advance of bureaucracy is intimately tied up with the expansion of capitalism. The link between the two is to be found in what Weber calls 'rational-legal' norms. One of the distinctive features of capitalist economic enterprise, according to Weber, is its routinised character: production depends upon the calculation of profit and expenditure, in relation to the input of raw materials and labour-power, and to the output of goods. This routinised form can be created only by the adoption of impersonal rules which specify procedure and make possible exact economic calculation. For Weber it was not fortuitous that the origins of capitalist enterprise in Europe coincided with the invention of double-entry bookkeeping; this was the concrete means of economic calculation necessary to routinised economic activity.

Rational-legal norms may guide capitalist enterprise but, according to Weber, they have much broader application to the administration of bureaucratic organisations in general. In the state, they are epitomised in the formation of an apparatus of formal, codified law; in other organisations, by formalised rules of procedure of various sorts. A bureaucratised organisation is distinguished by a number of specific traits. Weber's famous characterisation of these in his major work, *Economy and Society*, is as an 'ideal type' – a concept to which he accorded a basic role in his approach to the social sciences. An ideal type is a 'one-sided exaggeration' of certain aspects of reality, with which reality may then be compared. Thus Weber's ideal-typical formulation of bureaucracy lists a whole set of traits which will rarely, if ever, be found in fully developed form in any actual organisation. (See Max Weber, *Economy and Society*, Berkeley, University of California Press, 1978, vol. 2, pp. 956–94 [original German publication 1922].) It involves a pyramidal hierarchy of authority, arranged in terms of levels of official duties; bureaucratic officials are salaried, full-time staff, holding formal qualifications that are the condition of their appointment. There are two aspects of Weber's discussion of the connections between capitalism and bureaucracy that merit particular attention here. One concerns the consolidation of capitalist enterprise on a generalised basis. Weber lays considerably more stress than Marx does upon the early development of a bureaucratised state apparatus as a condition for the spread of capitalism. The formation of a system of law, and a guaranteed monetary system, administered by the state, was the necessary basis for the extension of capitalist production on a large scale.

The more significant feature of Weber's discussion, for my concerns in this chapter at any rate, bears rather upon the *consequences* of the association of capitalism, established as a generic type of society, with the advance of bureaucracy. It is here that Weber, as it were, throws down the gauntlet to Marxists, and challenges the thesis that a socialist society can generate a more democratic order than is possible in capitalist liberal democracy. Weber argues that bureaucracy and democracy stand in a paradoxical relation to one another. By its very nature, bureaucracy promotes the centralisation of power in the hands of a minority: those at the apex of the organisation. Marx regarded the expropriation of the mass of the population, in a capitalist society, from control of their means of production as the source both of exploitative class domination and of the limited character of bourgeois democracy. But of course all of this was to be transformed with the advent of socialism, via the abolition of private property and classes. Workers would recover control of their means of production; the sham freedom of 'free wage-labour' would cede place to real freedoms of democratised industry.

Weber's analysis places this conception in extreme jeopardy. The expropriation of workers from control of their means of production is not confined to the capitalist firm, and hence will not disappear with the transcendence of capitalism. According to Weber, loss of control over work processes – and the reduction of work to routinised operations, in which the majority are only 'cogs in a machine' – are characteristic of bureaucratisation in general. Industrial workers in a capitalist setting do not own, and have no formal control over, their means of production. But this is not specific to industry: the same is true of those at the lower levels of all bureaucratic organisations, such as large hospitals or universities – and it is true of participation in the government itself. The ideals of democracy, Weber emphasises, originated in small-scale societies in which those restricted segments of the population who were 'citizens' could assemble physically to exercise political power. But in the large-scale societies of contemporary times, in which citizenship rights have been extended to virtually everyone, this model of democracy becomes inapplicable. A modern democratic system presupposes a high level of bureaucratisation in the polity. To organise mass elections, there must be a firmly established 'rational-legal' system, accompanied by bureaucratised procedures ensuring that elections are properly co-ordinated and administered. Moreover, mass political parties also tend to become strongly bureaucratised, however open or democratic the goals to which they are supposedly dedicated. The modern era is one of 'party machine politics', in which the degree of participation of the ordinary citizen in the forging of political policies is strictly limited. Weber was one of the originators of what is sometimes called the theory of 'democratic elitism'. Modern democracy allows individuals a certain influence, through the franchise, over the elites who will rule them; but there can be no question of recapturing forms of 'participatory democracy' in which the population would have more extensive control over their destinies (see David Beetham, *Max Weber and the Theory of Modern Politics*, Cambridge, Polity Press, 1985).

Socialism in Weber's view would make things worse. For it would only further the spread of bureaucracy: the centralised direction of economic life inherent in socialist programmes would entail the development of a more heavily bureaucratised state than is characteristic of capitalist societies. Weber's assessment of capitalism and democracy is on the whole a pessimistic one. But he believed that liberal democracy sustains at least certain openings not covered by the enveloping tide of bureaucratisation. 'Democratic elitism' may be a limited form of political participation, but in the context of a multi-party system it is better than nothing. Moreover, although capitalism tends towards monopoly or oligopoly, it retains enough of a competitive character to permit freedoms of consumer choice that would become closed off where production is placed under central control.

Critical Comments

Weber's views must be taken very seriously, and certainly provide a sobering jolt to anyone inclined to suppose that, either through reform or revolution, the capitalist state can be readily transformed in the direction of securing higher levels of justice and freedom. But there are several reasons why his interpretation of the looming threat of bureaucratic domination cannot be accepted as it stands.

First, it seems mistaken to suppose, as Weber does, that the advance of bureaucracy produces a one-way movement of power away from those at the lower levels of organisations. Weber's student, Robert Michels (Robert Michels, *Political Parties*, London, Collier-Macmillan, 1968 [original German publication 1911]) generalised Weber's view in the shape of what he termed the 'iron law of oligarchy'. In Michels's words, 'who says organisation says oligarchy': in large-scale organisations power is necessarily concentrated in the hands of a few. But the iron law of oligarchy is neither an iron law nor even an accurate generalisation, expressed in unqualified form. Neither the increasing scale of societies or organisations within them (which Michels tended to place most emphasis upon), nor their increasing bureaucratisation (as stressed by Weber) lead inevitably to the consequences those authors suppose. This is, in fact, easy to demonstrate. Consider the following two examples, which are each very pertinent to my foregoing discussion of classes and the state. The modern economy is much more highly centralised than it was fifty years ago – due to the combination of factors I have mentioned, the growth of the megacorporations plus the increasing intrusion of the state into economic life. But some groups of workers have thereby gained much *more* power than they enjoyed previously, because they work in particularly strategic sectors of the economy. Workers in public utilities, or in energy production and distribution, for instance, are cases in point. Take as a second example workers on a highly integrated production line, in which control of the work process is presumptively taken wholly out of the workers' hands. Some writers, even including those of a Marxist persuasion (see especially Harry Braverman, *Labor and Monopoly Capital*, New York, Monthly Review Press, 1974) have reached the conclusion that such work settings 'sieve off' control of labour from the worker – thus reaching equally pessimistic conclusions to those of Weber and Michels. In fact, however, in highly co-ordinated work situations workers in certain respects acquire more power than they held before. For integrated production lines are particularly vulnerable to disruption by the co-ordinated action of small groups of workers.

Once more here we see the sociological importance of recognising that all social actors are knowledgeable agents, not merely the passive recipients of influences that irresistibly condition their conduct. The specific significance of this in such a context is that in bureaucratic organisations, including the state, there are more or less constant processes of the 'trading off' of resources. Power is usually a focus of active struggle, in which those in subordinate positions are by no means always the losers. To say this is not to write the views of Weber or Michels off as worthless, because there is no doubt that they point to tendencies which are common and real enough. But they are not universally associated either with bureaucracy or with the increasing scale of social organisation.

Weber's concentration upon problems of bureaucratic domination, I think, led him to underestimate the salience of Marx's critique of the capitalist state. The separation of the 'political', in which everyone is a citizen, from the 'economic' remains a distinctive feature of the advanced capitalist societies. The franchise, I have argued, has been a very important medium of generating change in these societies. It remains the case, however, that the power which industrial employees are able to wield in the sphere of industry is negative: it is founded upon the collective withdrawal of labour, or other modes of making their presence felt (controlling the flow of the production line, blocking its operation, or sabotaging it in other ways). Neither blue-collar workers nor lower-level white-collar employees have any formal rights of participation in the policies shaped from above.

If those in subordinate positions are already often able to sustain considerable power by negative means, there is good reason to suppose that such power might be further expanded by the extension of citizenship rights to the industrial sphere. In other words, the possibilities of achieving forms of 'participatory democracy' in contemporary societies should not be dismissed as unequivocally as Weber presumed. This applies with particular force to the industrial workplace, as follows from Marx's analysis. But it is difficult to deny that Marx, and many subsequent Marxists also, have been much too sanguine about how modes of participatory democracy might be successfully institutionalised in an anticipated socialist order. Existing socialist societies in Eastern Europe (with partial exceptions, such as Yugoslavian experiments with workers' self-management, and the activities of Solidarity in Poland) have hardly blazed the way in this respect.

States, Social Movements, Revolutions

The history of modern states, from at least the eighteenth century onwards, has been intertwined with the influence of social movements. Social movements can be regarded as forms of collective action concerned with achieving basic transmutations in some aspect of the existing order in a society. Like the study of the state and bureaucracy, the sociology of social movements owes a good deal to the pioneering efforts of Max Weber. Weber emphasised the significance of the contrasts between the stable, regularised patterns of bureaucratic organisation, and the more amorphous and volatile character of mass movements which develop in challenge to the existing order. Social movements, in his view, are dynamic influences, which may frequently serve to thoroughly shake or dissolve pre-established modes of behaviour, stimulating very rapid sources of change.

Various highly important types of social movement have existed in pre-modern times. Thus Cohn has discussed the impact of 'millenarian movements' in the Middle Ages (Norman Cohn, *The Pursuit of the Millenium*, London, Mercury Books, 1962). Such movements had fundamentally religious aims, being inspired by the ambition of realising the reign of God on this Earth. Other forms of pre-modern social movement were much more secular in their aims. Thus in late medieval Europe there occurred many peasant uprisings, stimulated usually by food shortages or high taxes. There are quite clear distinctions between both religious and secular movements in traditional societies, and the social movements which have had dramatic influences upon the development of modern states over the past two centuries. These distinctions can be illuminated by a differentiation which some writers have made between movements of rebellion, on the one hand, and movements of social revolution on the other. The peasant uprisings just referred to were rebellions in the sense that, while they may often have sought to overthrow an existing group of nobles, or a monarch, they did not envisage thorough-going processes of institutional reform. Even the beliefs in the coming of the millenium, saturated with Biblical notions, carried little inference that reform of the prevailing system of power was either desirable or possible. Revolutionary movements, by contrast, have the aim of radical secular social transformation, and are by and large specifically associated with the modern period. Such movements have only arisen with the advent of the idea of universal citizenship rights, coupled with concepts of equality and democracy. These concepts have certain general roots in the Classical World, and begin to have something like a modern shape as early as the seventeenth century. But it is only from the late eighteenth century onwards that they have become conjoined in a systematic way to movements pressing for radical social and political innovation.

I have already in the first chapter mentioned the profound influence of the American and French revolutions on processes of change in the nineteenth and twentieth centuries. There is a basic sense in which everyone in the world today lives in 'revolutionary societies'. No society has escaped the impact of 'two great revolutions', and probably the majority of countries have experienced at least one major phase of political revolution at some point over the past two hundred years. Marxism, of course, has been bound up with this phenomenon in an integral way since the turn of the twentieth century. Most twentieth-century social revolutions have been influenced or inspired by Marxist thought in one version or another. Marxism is unlike any other theoretical perspective in the social sciences in just this respect – it has served as the medium for large-scale sequences of social change achieved through the formation of oppositional social movements.

Interpretations of the nature and consequences of social revolutions differ sharply – something which is unsurprising given the highly charged character of the topic. Among the more influential of perspectives on social revolution and revolutionary movements are those offered by Tilly and Skocpol (Charles Tilly, *From Mobilisation to Revolution*, Reading, Mass., Addison-Wesley, 1978; Theda Skocpol, *States and Social Revolutions*, Cambridge, Cambridge University Press, 1979). Tilly has sought to analyse processes of revolutionary change within the framework of a general account of the mobilising of social movements in modern times. Characteristic of a world infused with notions of political involvement and participation is the tendency of groups actively to mobilise to promote their interests and their ideals. Social movements are means of mobilising group resources where these are either fragmented within a particular political order, or are actively repressed by the state authorities.

In Tilly's view, revolutionary movements are a sub-type of collective action in circumstances of what he sees as 'multiple sovereignty' – that is, where the state, for one reasons or another, does not have full control over the domain which supposedly it governs. Situations of multiple sovereignty can arise as a result of external war, or as a result of internal political clashes, or both. Thus the Russian Revolution of 1917 occurred in a context in which the involvement of the state in the First World War had resulted in lost territories and brought about deep internal political schisms. Revolutionary movements tend to gain momentum in conditions of multiple sovereignty if an incumbent government attempts to sustain its power by coercive means. This may often be connected to a sudden unwillingness, or incapacity, of the government to provide for needs that large sections of the population have previously assumed the state will cater for. For instance, in Italy following the end of the First World War, the rapid demobilisation of over two million men, together with a precipitous removal of wartime controls on food supplies and prices, set the stage for the burgeoning of radical movements on both Right and Left.

The main thrust of Skocpol's views is rather different. Tilly tends to assume that revolutionary movements are guided by the conscious, purposive pursuit of interests, and that 'successful' modes of revolutionary change occur when they manage to realise these interests. Skocpol sees such movements as typically more ambiguous and vacillating in their objectives, and large-scale revolutionary change as largely an unintended consequence of more partial aims that groups and movements strive towards. Social revolutions in modern world history – Skocpol concentrates upon the French, Russian and Chinese Revolutions – derive from the emergence of certain structural conditions of change within a particular pre-existing governmental regime. She also stresses in particular the importance of the international context in the creation of circumstances that can lead to social revolution. Her thesis is that revolutionary crises occurred, in each of the main instances she studies, when established governments, which in all three cases were autocratic monarchies, failed to meet the demands of changing international situations, where that failure was exacerbated by class divisions internally. The state authorities were not able to put through programmes of internal reform, or promote rapid economic development, sufficient to meet military threats from other states which had successfully achieved these changes. The resultant strains accentuated developing internal tensions in such a way as to cause the existing state structure to break apart – producing persistent political crises which developing social movements managed to exploit. The emergence of revolutionary situations, in Skocpol's words, did not occur

> because of deliberate activities to that end, either on the part of avowed revolutionaries or on the part of politically powerful groups within the Old Regimes. Rather revolutionary political crises, culminating in administrative and political breakdowns, emerged because the imperial states became caught in cross-pressures between intensified military competition or intrusions from abroad and constraints imposed on monarchical responses by the existing agrarian class structures and political institutions. (Skocpol, p. 285.)

Skocpol is no doubt right to emphasise that major social revolutions are not just the end-result of purposively organised movements directed towards overthrowing the existing order of things. But she probably draws too much of an opposition between purposive forms of social change and those that result from 'structural' dislocations. Her position and that of Tilly may be less discrepant than she seems to imagine. For modern social movements in general, and revolutionary movements in particular, *do* involve an unusually strong, and very potent, co-ordination of human activities in the service of collective purposes or interests. History cannot necessarily be bent to these purposes, but it is in the interaction between such forms of social mobilisation and their unforeseen consequences that many features of today's world have been forged.

5

The City: Urbanism and Everyday Life

Pre-Capitalist and Modern Cities

Consider again at this point the recency of the changes
that have transformed the contemporary world. Capitalist
enterprise upon a broad scale dates from only the sixteenth
century or so, and industrial capitalism from only the late
eighteenth century – and first of all in an isolated pocket
of the world at that. But the two hundred years since
1780 have witnessed more far-reaching transmutations in
social life than occurred in the vast span of human history
prior to that date. Nowhere is this more evident, as I
indicated in the first chapter of the book, than in the
character and spread of contemporary urbanism. In
grasping the impact of modern urbanism, the historical
aspect of the sociological imagination is especially
significant. There is an important sense, as I shall try to
indicate below, in which urbanism has become the milieu
in which all of us, in the advanced capitalist societies,
live. Hence it is very difficult for us to recapture a sense
of how social life used to be for human beings even two
centuries ago – although there remain large parts of the
world in which traditional styles of life continue to prevail.

In pre-modern civilisations, the city was normally
clearly differentiated from the countryside. It is certainly

possible to exaggerate the characteristics that pre-modern cities had in common. (For an example, see Gideon Sjoberg, *The Preindustrial City*, Glencoe, The Free Press, 1960. Although it has been widely criticised, this book remains something of a minor classic in its field, and contains a good deal of valuable material.) But some distinctive features appear in cities in most forms of society prior to the development of capitalism. Cities were ordinarily walled, the walls emphasising their enclosed character and their separation from the country-side, and also serving the purpose of military defence. The central area of traditional cities was usually occupied by the temple, palace, and market-place, this ceremonial and commercial centre sometimes being protected by a second, inner wall. Cities were the focus of science, the arts, and a cosmopolitan culture. But these were always the prerogative of small elites. Although cities may have been connected by a sophisticated road system, travel was usually also limited to the few, or mainly directed to military and trading activities. Within pre-capitalist cities, the pace of life was slow, and the common people usually tended to follow similar traditions to their counterparts living in the countryside. And, as I have mentioned earlier, cities were by contemporary standards very small.

The world's population has grown massively over the past two centuries – and continues to do so – and large numbers of this newly expanded population are packed into cities (see p. 6, above). The statistics are truly remarkable. There are something like 1,700 cities in the world today whose inhabitants number more than 100,000 persons. There exist about 250 cities having populations greater than the largest cities known to history until recent times, that is, with more than 500,000 inhabitants. The most populous cities number some 14 million inhabitants. But cities no longer have walls, and in the most extensive urban conglomerations administrative demarcations frequently cease to correspond to any real divisions in the urban sprawl. If contemporary economies are dominated by the megacorporations, urban life is overshadowed by the enveloping 'megalopolis', the 'city of cities'. The word is actually of Classical origin, having been coined by Peloponnesian statesmen-philosophers who planned a new city-state designed to be the envy of all civilisation. In its current usage, it has very little in common with this dream. The term was first applied in modern times to the Northeastern seaboard of the United States, a more or less continuous chain of urbanised areas covering some 450 miles from north of Boston to below Washington, D.C. Here there exist about 40 million people, living at a density of over 700 per square mile. Almost as large and dense an urban population is concentrated in the Great Lakes area of the United States and Canada.

The significance of these developments is not purely quantitative, in spite of a strongly marked tendency in some of the literature in urban sociology to presume so. That is to say, many writers have spoken of the urbanisation associated with industrial capitalism as though it were simply a movement of population from rural areas to cities. Of course it was such; but this movement was also part of a much more embracing set of changes altering the nature of urbanism itself – symbolised perhaps more than anything by the disappearance of the city walls. The implications of these comments will become clear if we look briefly at certain of the theories that have been at the forefront of urban analysis in sociology.

The Views of the 'Chicago School'

Until quite recently, the contributions of the 'Chicago school' of sociology, which was prominent in the first two decades of this century, have tended to dominate debates about urban studies. Two related conceptions of the Chicago school are worthy of particular attention. One is the so-called 'ecological approach' to the distribution of city neighbourhoods. This was originally worked out on the basis of an explicit analogy with ecological processes in biology: processes whereby the vegetation and animal life in the physical environment become distributed in an orderly fashion, via the modes of their adaptation to that environment. R. E. Park described the application of this standpoint to the city as follows. The city, he wrote, 'is, it seems, a great sorting and sifting mechanism, which, in ways that are not yet wholly understood, infallibly selects out of the population as a whole the individuals best suited to live in a particular region and a particular milieu' (Robert E. Park, *Human Communities*, Glencoe, The Free Press, 1952, p. 79). The city is ordered into 'natural areas' via processes of competition, invasion, and succession comparable to those which occur in biological ecology. These processes govern the 'zoning' of the characteristics of different neighbourhood areas. The central area of cities tends to have a heavy concentration of business, commercial establishments, and entertainments. Distributed around this in the 'inner city' there are likely to be decaying neighbourhoods having a high proportion of cheap apartments or lodging houses. Farther out there will be stable working-class areas, with middle-class suburbia at the outermost fringes.

The ecological approach is often thought to be concerned with urbanism only in the contemporary societies. Such is not the case with the second influential standpoint linked to the Chicago school, Louis Wirth's discussion of 'urbanism as a way of life', which lays some claim to identifying universal characteristics of life in cities. Wirth's views have occasionally been almost caricatured by his critics, so it is important to try to describe them accurately. His ideas are summed up in a celebrated article first published in 1938 (Louis Wirth, 'Urbanism as a way of life', *American Journal of Sociology*, vol. 44, 1938. See also A. J. Reiss, *Louis Wirth on Cities and Social Life*, Chicago, University of Chicago Press, 1964). Wirth distinguishes three characteristics as pertaining to cities in general: size, density, and heterogeneity of population. In cities, large numbers of people live in close proximity to one another, but the majority do not know each other personally. He recognised that these criteria have a largely formal character, and that their consequences are shaped by a variety of factors. None the less, he did see such consequences as involving a specific style of life characteristic of city-dwellers. In cities, many contacts with others are fleeting and fragmentary, and treated by those concerned as instrumental, as means to ends rather than as satisfying relationships in themselves. The individual, Wirth says, is stripped of the 'spontaneous self-expression, the morale, and the sense of participation that comes from living in an integrated society' (Wirth, p. 13). Following the ecological view, Wirth argues that large, dense populations inevitably lead to diversification and specialisation of areas: as with plant and animal life, differentiation of function allows greater numbers of individuals to live together in a relatively small area. The dissolution of an 'integrated society' in the city entails the prevalence of orderly routines, controlled by impersonally defined rules of behaviour; one should note here a definite similarity with Weber's characterisation of bureaucracy.

Wirth qualified his views in several respects. The urban

'way of life' is not necessarily confined to those who actually live in cities of any size, because the influence of cities spreads to affect more far-flung populations. The reverse also holds. Not all of those who live in cities are absorbed into their anonymous routines. Immigrants from rural areas may preserve strong aspects of their pre-established ways of living; and some of these features may be sustained in the long term. Moreover, Wirth does not take the traits he describes to be in any way exhaustive of the characteristics of city life, but a minimum specification. He insists on this point, however, partly because he wishes to formulate an account of cities that will have very broad application, and that will not be limited to modern urbanism.

There are many ways in which both Wirth's views and the ecological approach have been criticised. Here I shall confine myself to a critical evaluation relevant to the broader themes of this book; and I shall be concerned to point to aspects of these two sets of ideas which, appropriately reformulated, retain their validity today. My critical comments can be grouped into four categories, and I shall concentrate them mainly upon Wirth's thesis.

First, Wirth's theory certainly does not have the general application claimed for it. Based mainly on observations of American cities in the 1920s and 1930s, it has definite limitations even as applied to urbanism in industrial capitalism. But it is especially deficient when applied to cities in pre-capitalist societies. There has been a considerable amount of recent comparative research upon urbanism in such societies, in archaeology and anthropology. While the results are not easy to generalise, I think that by and large these bear out what Sjoberg, in his book mentioned earlier, describes as his 'principal hypothesis': 'that in their structure, or form, pre-industrial cities – whether in mediaeval Europe, traditional China,

India, or elsewhere – resemble one another closely and in turn differ markedly from modern industrial-urban centres' (Sjoberg, p. 5). The differences concern features of pre-modern cities mentioned three or four pages earlier. Compared with large modern urban areas, traditional cities were very compact, walled, having a stable distribution of neighbourhoods surrounding a clearly defined ceremonial and marketing area.

Second, it is mistaken to suppose, as Wirth seems to do, that a generalised account of urbanism can be based solely upon the characteristics of cities themselves. Cities both express and encapsulate aspects of the wider society of which they are a part. This remark meshes closely with the first. In pre-capitalist societies there are certain respects in which life in cities parallels that in rural areas. In both the influence of tradition is strong, even among the more cosmopolitan elites; most relationships are personalised rather than being of the anonymous type Wirth portrays. But in other respects, the contrasts between city and countryside are much greater than they are in modern societies; indeed, as I shall point out shortly, in contemporary societies, such contrasts virtually lose their significance. Cities do not merely exist 'in' pre-modern societies. In their various and complex relations with the countryside, they are crucial to the overall organisation of those societies. City: civilisation: state – these often appear with good reason as almost synonymous terms in the literature of archaeology and anthropology. The same general theorem holds for urbanism in modern societies. That is to say, the character of cities can be adequately analysed only in relation to the broader features of those societies as a whole. Here again the city is simultaneously a part of, and a major influence upon, the institutions of the overall society. But the character of urbanism today is very different from that in the pre-modern city, reflecting the profound nature of the social transformations brought about by the advent of capitalism.

Third, Wirth's formulations incorporate some of the more dubious elements of the theory of industrial society – even though he specifically sets out to develop an approach relevant to cities in all types of society. The theory of industrial society, as I have pointed out previously, in its various versions, involves a dichotomous conception of social change, contrasting 'traditional' with 'industrial society'. Such dichotomous conceptions, whether or not they have specifically used the term 'industrial society', have been very influential in the social sciences. One of the most well known of such notions was coined by the German thinker Ferdinand Tönnies at around the turn of the century. He spoke of a general movement of society from *Gemeinschaft* (community) to *Gesellschaft* (association). *Gemeinschaft* is the equivalent of Wirth's small community, or 'integrated society', dominated by 'spontaneous self-expression'. *Gesellschaft*, involving impersonal, instrumental social relationships, increasingly replaces *Gemeinschaft* with the development of modern, large-scale societies. Wirth drew upon Tönnies's ideas – among others, especially those of Georg Simmel – in establishing his analysis of urbanism. In his hands it retains something of a developmental slant – since in the contemporary societies, urbanism becomes ever more predominant – but the greater weight is placed upon translating it into a contrast between the rural and the urban. However, this leads to a double set of limitations. One is that I have just referred to: the equation of *Gesellschaft* with urbanism in general does not work, for pre-modern societies are for the most part distinctively different from contemporary urbanism. But Wirth's conception of urbanism can also be fruitfully criticised by contrasting it to ideas drawn from the alternative general standpoint offered by Marxism. In fact, some of the most significant recent contributions to the analysis of contemporary urbanism are to be found in recent writings indebted to Marxism. These, as I shall try to indicate, help illuminate *why* some of the elements of urbanism Wirth identifies are specific to the contemporary era.

Finally, Wirth's approach, especially in so far as it involves the ecological analogy, displays the limitations of a 'naturalistic' model of sociology. The ecological system of city neighbourhoods is seen as being formed, as Park explicitly says, through a series of 'natural processes' that occur like impersonal events in the physical world. Seen in this way, such processes appear to have an unchangeable character, like laws of nature. Quite a different view emerges if we analyse urbanism in terms of the standpoint I outlined in the introductory chapters.

Urbanism and Capitalism

How should we characterise the overall qualities of the contrasts between pre-modern cities and capitalist urbanism? An answer to this question, I have emphasised, must relate urbanism to the broader characteristics of societies, and therefore to the general social transformations brought about by the formation and development of capitalism. In pre-capitalist societies, the city was the centre of state power, and of a limited range of productive and commercial operations; the vast majority of the population were engaged in agrarian occupations. The emergence of capitalism, and its consolidation as industrial capitalism, involved a wholesale movement of population from rural to urban milieux. But this was both brought about by, and further stimulated, profound changes in the nature of the 'urban'. One indicator of this, in the initial development of industrial capitalism in Britain in the late eighteenth century, is that most of the early manufacturing centres were not located in the established larger cities. Manchester offers one of the most striking examples of urban expansion. In 1717 it was a town numbering some 10,000 people; by 1851, as the focus of manufacture and commerce over a broad area of Lancashire, it encompassed a population of some 300,000. By the opening of the twentieth century, spilling out into surrounding towns, the population of the Manchester area was 2,400,000. Such observations document that the driving impetus to the spread of urbanism in the late eighteenth and nineteenth centuries differs dramatically from the factors underlying previous forms of urbanism. But they do not disclose the specific character of the new urbanism.

We can perhaps best illuminate to traits of contemporary urbanism, and its relation to capitalist development, via the concept of what Marx called 'commodification'. I have already referred to this notion when discussing Offe's interpretation of the capitalist state. According to Marx, the notion of commodification is basic to the analysis of the capitalist order: the buying and selling of goods, including labour-power, in order to generate profit, is what capitalist enterprise is all about. We should not be surprised to find, therefore, that commodification extends to the very milieux in which human beings live. We can make sense of modern urbanism, and the styles of social life associated with it, by seeing how *space itself becomes commodified* in capitalist societies. In pre-capitalist societies, although there was a great deal of variation, in city and countryside alike land and housing were either not alienable, or were subject to restrictions upon their alienability. ('Alienable' here means that property can be transferred by some mode of payment from one owner to another.) With the advent of capitalism, however, land and buildings become freely alienable, as commodities that can be bought and sold on the market.

The commodification of space entangles the physical milieu in the productive system of capitalism as a whole. This has several implications:

(1) Capitalist urbanism becomes a 'created environment' which dissolves previous divisions between the city and countryside. The pre-capitalist city existed in a dependent relationship with, yet was clearly demarcated from, the countryside. But in capitalism, industry spans the city–countryside division. Agriculture becomes capitalised and mechanised, and brought under the sway of similar socio-economic factors to those that prevail in other sectors of production. In conjunction with this process, differences in modes of social life between countryside and city also become progressively undermined. In so far as space is a social, and not purely a physical, phenomenon, 'city' and 'countryside', as such, cease to exist. In their stead, there is a differentiation between the 'built environment' and the environment of 'open space'. (This is discussed in an interesting way in David Harvey, *Social Justice and the City*, London, Arnold, 1973.)

(2) In all pre-capitalist societies, human beings lived close to nature – and in many cultures have conceived of themselves as participating in the natural world in ways that have become completely alien in the West. But the built environment of capitalist societies draws a radical separation between human life and nature. This is the case in the first instance in the capitalistic workplace, in which both the character of the labour task and the physical setting of factory or office sever human beings from the influence of the soil, weather, or cycle of the seasons. The situating of the workplace in an urban milieu of commodified space, moreover, strongly reinforces this.

Most of us today spend most of our lives in settings that are almost wholly of human manufacture.

(3) The phenomena that affect the distribution of neighbourhoods are tied to general features of the capitalist societies, and at the same time lend an extra dimension to them. This comment may sound a truism, but is actually of some importance in relation to recent discussions of the city influenced by Marxism. Some authors have forcibly expressed the view that there can be no such thing as 'urban sociology', for reasons to do with the first two points I have made above. If the created environment is an integral feature of capitalist society, then its analysis can be directly derived from an under-standing of that form of society as a whole. I have a good deal of sympathy with this view, since it does seem to me to be the case that the phenomena I have discussed in previous chapters – capitalist production, class conflict, and the state – are all directly bound up with the transformation of the 'urban' into the 'built environment'.

These things being granted, however, it still seems necessary to formulate concepts that will analyse capitalist urbanism in such a way as to show what form such connections with the overall society take. Rex's formu-lation of what he calls a 'theory of housing classes' is an endeavour to do just this (see John Rex and Robert Moore, *Race, Community and Conflict*, Oxford, Oxford University Press, 1967; and other publications by Rex). Rex's ideas were worked out specifically as an attempt to provide a more satisfactory account of neighbourhood organisation, and city growth, than that offered by the Chicago sociologists. The ecological approach, Rex emphasises, depends upon too mechanical a view of the ecological processes which supposedly determine the characteristics of city neighbourhoods. He tries to replace it with a perspective which gives due recognition to the active attempts of city-dwellers to influence the milieux in which they live. Since his discussion is based on British materials, it also provides a useful counterbalance to the tendency of the 'Chicago school' – and a goodly amount of urban analysis since – to depend overmuch upon American research.

His beginning-point is the mushrooming of industrial settlements in Britain in the nineteenth century; he takes the growth of Birmingham as a particular example. In the earlier phases of development of such settlements, patterns of residential distribution tended to be very directly influenced by the perceived needs of employers. The homes of industrialists and other local dignitaries were built in areas having good access to central facilities but avoiding the grime and soot of the factories. While cottage industry still played a major role in production (well into the nineteenth century) employers were in part relieved of the need to provide workers' accommodation. But they did build such accommodation to an increasing extent; some set up barracks for workers only, but mostly they built rows of workers' family cottages, distributed around the factories or near the railways. No attempt was made to capture elements of the communal life of the traditional agricultural villages, although communal cultures – of adversity – rapidly developed.

In the late nineteenth and early twentieth centuries, this 'direct class division' in housing broke down. The sheer expansion of industry, population, and urban areas provided the backdrop to this. But there were other, more specific factors. Provision for housing by employers kept capital static that might be otherwise invested more profitably; tied housing also restricted the mobility of employees. Important too, however, was the development of a more differentiated class system, with demand for superior dwellings to the old workers' cottages coming from skilled and white-collar workers. Thus the provision of work became separated from the provision of housing and other municipal facilities, these latter tasks being taken over by specialised building firms of varying sizes. Such homes, financed through mortgages, have consistently been mostly owner-occupied.

Since the early part of the twentieth century, then, there has come about the expansion of *housing markets*, connected to industrial and financial capital, on the one hand, and to labour markets, on the other. It is in these terms that we can seek to understand the 'ecological' patterns of movement and neighbourhood segregation noted by the Chicago researchers. They result, according to Rex, from struggle for scarce and desired types of housing, clustering residents into 'housing classes'. In the larger cities, we can distinguish several housing classes. These include, among others, people who own outright, and live in, houses in the most desirable areas; those who 'own' such houses through mortgage borrowing; those in other mortgaged owner-occupied dwellings in less desirable areas; persons in privately rented accommodation; and people living in rented accommodation provided by the state. In many cities, those in the most affluent housing classes have moved out of the city centre, into favoured inner-city suburbs, or sometimes outside the city altogether. The less privileged mortgaged owner-occupiers have also sought to move away from the inner city, helping to create a drive towards the ever-widening spread of the outer suburbs. The working class, with the exception of some groupings of skilled workers, mostly live in rented housing owned by the state, in housing tracts often located quite close to the inner city.

The attainment of state-provided housing on an extensive basis is one aspect of the struggles of labour movements described in previous chapters. In most countries socialist or labour parties have taken the initiative in developing and maintaining such housing, although it is normally actually built by private contractors. Qualification for public housing and for the securing of mortgages, Rex argues, are two main areas of class struggle over housing. Most people wish to own their homes, and will seek to gain a mortgage loan if possible. However, those in secure and better-paid jobs, particularly white-collar jobs, are likely both to be more prepared to invest a substantial proportion of their income in a mortgage, and to qualify to attain one. But public housing is also involved in struggle, for provision rarely meets demand. Groups who are able to acquire tenancy of public housing are likely to defend, or seek to extend, the system of allocation whereby they were able to gain such tenancy.

Those who are in public housing are normally by no means the least advantaged within urban class struggles. In competition with them are groups denied access both to mortgage loans and to state-provided dwellings, and who are forced therefore to rent in the private sector – often in circumstances where they are highly vulnerable to manipulation by unscrupulous landlords, because they are without the forms of rent control or protection which residents in public housing enjoy. These groups are likely to find themselves in what the Chicago sociologists called 'zones of transition': seedy or slum areas, usually on the fringes of the business and entertainment districts of the inner city. Zones of transition contain a high proportion of individuals living in small, overcrowded apartments or lodging-houses, and are also likely to be areas to which newly arrived immigrants perforce tend to gravitate. For immigrants, subject to racial discrimination, however, these areas may be much less transitional than for other groups. This is most marked in American cities with the development of more or less permanent ghettos, but a similar phenomenon on a lesser scale is found in several other countries in which there are racial minorities clearly distinguishable from the majority of the population. In the United States the black ghetto developed in the wake of migration from South to North, starting in the years prior to the First World War (see A. Meier and E. M. Rudwick, *From Plantation to Ghetto*, New York, Hill & Wang, 1966). There are major differences between white and black patterns of mobility within urban areas. White moves are frequently long-distance: from one neighbourhood to another quite separate from it within a city, or between cities geographically far removed from one another. Black moves on average area of much shorter distance. As expressed in the 'flight to the suburbs of whites in the 1950s and 1960s', this contrast lies behind the continuing deterioration of inner-city areas. Since ghettos in a certain sense thus tend to be stable areas, with cultural traits distinguishing them from other neighbourhoods, ethnic and spatial segregation becomes tightly meshed (see the classic work, Gerald Suttles, *The Social Order of the Slum*, Chicago, University of Chicago Press, 1968). The stabilising of urban ghetto areas, notwithstanding high rates of individual movement within them, poses formidable problems for those who wish to escape. But such areas can also thereby become the locales of new urban protest movements, which can perhaps also recreate communal relations of reciprocity only weakly developed in the more affluent urban areas.

The type of account that can be developed on the basis of Rex's arguments seems to me to be essentially correct. Locating the distribution of urban neighbourhoods in the active struggles of groups in housing markets emphasises factors of generalised importance in the capitalist societies. A number of further comments however, have to be made. I do not think it particularly useful to speak, as Rex does, of 'housing classes'. It is right to stress that urban conflicts are often every bit as chronic and intense as conflicts in the industrial sphere, and that housing markets have their own specific features which cannot be directly reduced to the latter. But rather than regarding urban struggles as involving 'housing classes' distinguishable from the rest of the class system, it seems preferable to treat such conflicts as contributing to the overall character of the class structure of a given society. We can then see different modes of neighbourhood organisation, and styles of life, as consolidating some aspects of class divisions, while cutting across others. Differential availability of mortgages, for example, may tend to reinforce divisions between manual and non-manual workers, in so far as those in secure white-collar occupations are likely to have a predominant share in available mortgage financing. Patterns of residential segregation tending to cluster groups subject to ethnic discrimination in areas separate from the bulk of the indigenous working class, on the other hand, may be an important source of schism within the working class as a whole.

Rex's discussion is based upon British materials, and, as he accepts, we have to be as circumspect in generalising from these as from American research. The depredation of the inner city has proceeded further in most large urban areas in the United States than has been the case in Europe. This is undoubtedly partly due to the greater impact of urban planning in most European countries, and to more extensive provision of public housing in the latter. If these variations were to be examined in any detail, we should have to look at the ways in which the state, and industrial and financial capital, together with the activities of residents, interact in different patterns. It is not difficult to see the relevance of Offe's discussion of the state to such an undertaking. For the factors producing the commodified space of modern urbanism are constantly counterbalanced by processes of de-commodification. The provision of public housing, urban planning, rent and investment controls, and the fostering of communal facilities such as parks and recreational amenities are all relevant here.

It is a very important question how far the traits of urbanism portrayed in the preceding pages are specific to capitalist societies and how far they are generic to any type of modern social order which has reached a certain level of industrialisation. This question is of course one aspect of the more overarching theme introduced early on in the book: whether industrialised societies tend to have similar features whatever their origins and trajectories of development.

In recent years a number of studies of urban organisation in Eastern Europe have appeared, allowing at least some degree of purchase on the issue. Several of the main features involved in processes analysed by Rex are not found, or exist in sharply contrasting form, in East European urbanism. Urban land is mostly controlled in an extensive fashion by the state, and housing markets are considerably more restricted than in the West. Dwellings are constructed by companies that are either a direct part of the governmental apparatus, or closely monitored by it. What determines where individuals live is not primarily influenced by how much they can afford to pay; and there is not complete freedom of mobility from city to city or area to area. Szelinyi tells a story about a research colleague in Hungary working on housing issues, with whom Szelinyi exchanged notes and research reports. After reading Szelinyi's account of his research and its implications, he asked in a puzzled way, 'Do you recommend that people ought to live where they want to live?' The idea both surprised and upset him, because if individuals follow their own inclinations as to the type of house they want, and where they want it to be situated, what would there be left for the government planners to do? (Ivan Szelinyi, *Urban Inequalities Under State Socialism*, New York, Oxford University Press, 1983, p. 14.)

Of course, there are central and local government regulations restraining various aspects of housing development and neighbourhood zoning in all Western societies too. There is also city planning in greater or lesser degree. But the scope and nature of such regulations and planning allows housing markets to flourish in conditions of relative freedom of individual movement. Decisions that in the West are governed by prices and ability to pay are in Eastern Europe controlled by urban management.

On the basis of his research in Hungary, and comparisons with other East European societies, Szelinyi is able to document some systematic differences between cities West and East. Post-war schemes of housing reconstruction in Hungary were based on the presumption that housing is not a commodity, so that rents should not necessarily be related to quality of dwellings. Rent, it was held, should only be a quite small element of household expenditure; families (not individuals) should have a right to housing independent of their capability to pay particular rents.

The result is a distribution of housing types, and of urban neighbourhoods, substantially different from most Western cities. Dwellings built by private contractors and bought and sold on the market (a minority of the total housing stock) are largely in the hands of those in lower income groups. Those of higher status, such as government officials or professionals, tend to live in apartments owned and maintained by the state. Among those who paid anything for their houses, which the more affluent are less likely to do, the higher socio-economic groups have paid less while getting superior housing. Such a situation arises from credit and exchange policies favouring governmental officials, plus the fact that the higher income groups tend disproportionately to have inherited superior housing from the pre-war years.

Neighbourhood zones in capitalist societies develop mainly via the market values of housing stock and land. In Eastern Europe, city zoning is influenced much more strongly by administrative decisions. This does not mean that strong differentiation between what Rex calls housing classes does not exist; but the mechanisms of allocation again are different from most Western cities. There are deteriorating areas, but these do not tend to cluster around the city centre, as is frequently the case in the West, especially in the United States. Most central city land is owned by the state, and around the city centres there are often areas with superior housing stock, the transitional zones lying further out. Neighbourhoods tend to be much more homogeneous in terms both of the character of ownership and style of housing than in Western cities.

These findings reinforce the point made earlier, that the differentiation of city areas and housing types is not a 'natural process', but is tied to broader aspects of social organisation. At the same time, it is scarcely plausible to claim that there are not processes affecting the development of urban life in all modern cities. The urbanism of Eastern Europe is as distinct from the traditional city as that of the West. It is therefore appropriate in concluding this chapter to shift back to a more general level.

Urbanism and Everyday Life

While Wirth's characterisation of 'urbanism as a way of life' may be strictly limited in its relevance to cities in general, it is arguable that it does illuminate important aspects of modern urbanism as a whole. Perhaps we can best express this, however, by saying that the advent of the modern city fosters a texture of day-to-day life quite different from that prevailing in traditional societies. In the latter, the influence of custom is always strong, and even in cities daily life for the majority of the population has a *moral* character to it: as do the connections of day-to-day life with crises and transitions in personal existence – with sickness and death, and the cycle of the generations. There are moral frameworks, usually anchored in religion, that offer ready-to-hand modes of confronting or coping with these phenomena in conformity with traditionally established practices.

The processes involved in the disintegration of such practices are complex and variable. But there can be no doubt that the characteristic forms of day-to-day life fostered by the expansion of modern urbanism are very different from those in preceding types of society. Here it seems useful to follow Lefebvre in speaking of the emergence of a distinct form of 'everyday life' which has a strongly routinised character, stripped of moral meaning and of what he calls the 'poetry of life'. Most of what we do in the course of our day-to-day lives, in modern societies, is strictly functional in nature. This applies, for example, to the clothes we wear, the daily routines we follow, and to most of the features of the buildings in which we live and work. By contrast, in Lefebvre's words: 'With the Incas, the Aztecs, in Greece or in Rome, every detail (gestures, words, tools, utensils, costumes etc.) bears the imprint of a *style*; nothing had as yet become prosaic . . . the prose and the poetry of life were still identical.' The spread of capitalism ensured the pre-eminence of the 'prose of the world' – the primacy of the economic, the instrumental, and the technical – such that 'it involves everything – literature, art and objects and all the poetry of existence has been evicted' (Henri Lefebvre, *Everyday Life in the Modern World*, London, Allen Lane, 1971, p. 29).

It would be a mistake to see this as portraying an unrealistically romanticised view of pre-modern societies. What Lefebvre is getting at is the replacement of morally grounded tradition, integrated with broader aspects of human existence, by narrowly focused routines. Two sets of factors are especially important in giving rise to the empty or banal character of everyday life in the modern world. One concerns the specific form of commodified space in the 'built environment' of modern urbanism: the built environment is denuded of aesthetic form. The second is what some social analysts have referred to as the 'sequestration' of types of human activity and experience which in prior types of society were in full view, and inherent in the fabric of social life for the whole community.

The practice of locking up criminals in prisons in punishment for their wrong-doings, for example, is only a development of the past two centuries or so. Gaols existed in medieval Europe, but were mainly used for the custody of suspects prior to sentencing, or for debtors. Serious crimes were punished by means of banishment, hanging, or the inflicting of physical pain, rather than by imprisonment (Michael Ignatieff, *A Just Measure of Pain*, London, Macmillan, 1978). Not simply prisons, but mental asylums and medical hospitals have come to exist extensively, and to be clearly separated from one another also, only during the same period. Sequestration refers to the removal from everyday life of those sorts of phenomena which threaten its continuity: crime, madness, illness, and death. Such phenomena, and the individuals most involved with them, are separated from the flow of everyday life of the majority. The 'prose of life', the routine of daily activity directed to instrumental ends, thereby finds a further extension.

These observations suggest some of the ways in which the overall organisation of societies is tied to intimate features of our daily lives. One of the most important contributions of sociology lies in allowing us to understand the nature of such ties. For what we may think of as the most intensely personal aspects of our experience both shape, and are shaped by, influences from which they might at first sight seem quite remote. This point is well illustrated by the study of the family and sexuality, to which I turn in the next chapter.

6

The Family and Gender

During the period – the 1950s and 1960s – at which the
theory of industrial society enjoyed pre-eminence as
a framework for social analysis, a specific type of
interpretation of the development of the family tended
to prevail in the sociological literature. Expressed rather
crudely, this interpretation ran as follows. Prior to
industrialisation, the family was deeply embedded in a
broad set of kinship relations ('the extended family') and
was the hub of economic production. The transition to
an industrial society, however, in which the family is no
longer, as such, a unit of production, dissolved the
extended family. Kinship relations became pared down
to the 'nuclear family': the parental couple and their
immediate offspring. 'The family,' as one observer put it,
'has become *a more specialised agency than before*,
probably more specialised than it has been in any
previously known society' (Talcott Parsons, 'The American family', in T. Parsons and R. F. Bales, *Family,
Socialisation and Interaction Process*, London, Routledge
& Kegan Paul, 1956, p. 10). Most writers who proposed
this view, none the less, including Parsons, strongly
defended the continuing significance of the family (and
marriage) in contemporary society. The nuclear family
remains the focus for the procreation and upbringing of

children and, more than ever before, is a source of emotional support and satisfaction for its members.

This type of view has come under strong attack in recent years: so much so, in fact, that it is by now in certain respects substantially discredited. The study of the family is an area of social analysis that has been greatly altered by a series of concurrent developments over the past decade or so. The standpoint outlined above was for the most part only poorly informed by historical materials to do with forms of family relationship that existed prior to the present time. The work of historians of the family has demonstrated that some assumptions made by the earlier authors were, to say the least, quite suspect. A second source of ideas that has had a major impact upon pre-existing interpretations of the family has come from the work of feminist writers, some of whom have drawn extensively upon Marxist thought.

Changes in Family Structure

It is certainly the case that, in Western Europe prior to the development of capitalism in the seventeenth and eighteenth centuries, the family household was generally a productive unit. That is to say, production was carried on in the home or on the land adjacent to it, and all family members, including children, made contributions to productive activity. The expansion of capitalist enterprise, even before the advent of large-scale industry, undermined this situation by incorporating family members separately into labour markets. The subsequent widespread separation of the home from the workplace was the culmination of this process.

But it has proved mistaken to presume that these changes dissolved a pre-existing extended family system.

Historical research has indicated that, throughout most of Western Europe, the family had typically been closer to the nuclear than to the extended type for at least several centuries prior to the early formation of capitalism – although wider kin relations were certainly in some respect more important than today. Where the domestic group was larger, this was because of the presence of household servants. It has also become evident that the relations between the development of capitalism and the character of family life were considerably more complex than presumed in the view described previously. Early capitalist entrepreneurs, for instance, quite often employed families rather than individuals, conforming to the traditional expectation that children as well as adults should participate in productive labour. Although this led to the brutal exploitation of children, working in miserable conditions in mines or factories, it would be a half-truth to attribute it to the greed of employers. Provision of family employment was expected by those coming from agrarian backgrounds, in which the domestic group co-operated in production. The impulse to break down the economic solidarity of the family came largely from the employers themselves, in combination with liberal legislation prohibiting the use of child labour. Finally, and especially important, the forms of domestic life that tend to predominate today seem to have been influenced more by the bourgeois family, whose life style became in some part 'diffused downwards', than by the direct impact of capitalism upon the wage-worker.

While his work has met with some considerable criticism, and stands in need of some modification, Stone's analysis of the development of family life in England offers a useful classification of changes in domestic forms (Lawrence Stone, *The Family, Sex and Marriage in England 1500–1800*, London, Weidenfeld & Nicolson,

1977). He distinguishes three main phases in the development of the family over the three hundred years from the sixteenth to the early nineteenth centuries. In the sixteenth century, and for many years before, the predominant family type was what Stone calls the 'open lineage family'. Although centred upon the nuclear family, the domestic unit was caught up in broader community involvements, including those with other kin. Family relationships, like those in the community at large, were radically different from those prevailing at a later date. Marriage was not a focal point of emotive attachment or dependence, at any level of the class system. According to Stone:

> Conventional wisdom was that happiness could only be anticipated in the next world, not in this, and sex was not a pleasure but a sinful necessity justified only by the need to propagate the race. Individual freedom of choice ought at all times and in all respects to be subordinated to the interests of others, whether lineage, parents, neighbours, Church or state. As for life itself, it was cheap, and death came easily and often. The expectation of life was so low that it was imprudent to become too emotionally dependent upon any other human being. (Stone, p. 5.)

Here the author may be overstating his case; how far marital relations, and those between parents and children, were typically marked by the absence of strong emotional ties remains a matter of some debate among historians. But there is no doubt that concepts of romantic love flourished only in courtly circles, and were not associated with marriage and the family.

It does seem to have been generally true that neither relations between husband and wife, nor between parents and children, were especially intimate or affective. (The pioneer study on long-term changes in parent–child relations is Philippe Ariès, *Centuries of Childhood*, Harmondsworth, Penguin, 1973.) Marriage ties were not initiated through personal choice. Among those in the higher echelons of society, marriage was regarded as a means of securing the inheritance of property, or of achieving other forms of economic or political advantage. For peasants and artisans, marriage was usually a necessity for economic survival; among lower as among upper classes it was normal for the selection of partners to be made by others than the marital pair themselves. The relative dearth of emotional intimacy in the family was not expressed in the physical separation of individuals from one another. Far from it; in all classes of society people lived in circumstances in which personal privacy was very restricted, inside the household and outside. The distribution of rooms in dwellings to which the vast majority of those living in the contemporary capitalist societies are accustomed became common only in the eighteenth century and later. The dwellings of the rich may have had many rooms, but they were characteristically interconnected, without hallways; servants slept in the same rooms as or in close proximity to their masters. The peasantry and urban poor lived in houses with one or two rooms; even among the better off, rooms were shared, and not clearly demarcated as they later became in terms of their use. Not until the eighteenth century, as Ariès puts it, did the family begin 'to hold society at a distance', to 'push it back beyond a steadily extending zone of private life' (Ariès, p. 386). Beginning with those of the better off, houses came to be designed in their modern form, with halls allowing privacy, and with the living-rooms separated from the bedrooms.

Prior to such developments, according to Stone's portrayal, a second type of domestic life came into being, although only in certain social groups. This he calls, in a rather cumbersome way, the 'restricted patriarchal nuclear family'; it lasted from the early sixteenth to the opening of the eighteenth century. It was largely confined to the higher reaches of society, and was a transitional type, intervening between the older form and the emergence of the family in something like its modern guise. Loyalties which had previously connected the nuclear family to other kin and groupings in the local community became attenuated, and were replaced by allegiances to the state. The power of the male head of the household was strengthened inside the family, reflecting his secular power in the state; and the nuclear family became a more distinctly separated unity.

The rise of the 'closed domesticated nuclear family', the basis of family organisation that persists into the twentieth century, was marked by several distinctive traits. These Stone sums up by the term 'affective individualism'. The formation of ties of marriage became more and more a matter of personal selection for those involved, although developing within different characteristic patterns of courtship in different classes. Choice of a mate became increasingly influenced by the desire for a relationship offering affection or 'love', guided by norms that associated sexuality specifically with marriage. Relations between parents and children also developed a more strongly emotional content, in which a concern with the proper 'education' of children also came to the fore. The pre-eminence of this type of family in society as a whole did not come about as a simple, uninterrupted process of diffusion, however. There were various reversals and dislocations in the process.

Gender, Patriarchy, and Capitalist Development

One of the most important influences upon the sociology of the family in particular, but having broader implications for other fields of social analysis, has come from recent feminist writers. Feminists have been especially preoccupied with analysing the origins of patriarchy – the dominance of men over women within the family and in the context of other social institutions. Anthropological research indicates that all societies which have been reliably studied are patriarchal, although the degree and nature of male domination has varied considerably. I shall not be concerned here to discuss the problem of the ubiquity of patriarchy, however. (For a relevant and influential discussion, see Nancy Chodorow, *The Reproduction of Mothering*, Berkeley, University of California Press, 1978; for a survey of relevant anthropological evidence, which includes extensive discussion of Third World societies, see Barbara Rogers, *The Domestication of Women*, London, Kogan Page, 1980.)

The changes in the forms of the family described in the foregoing section led to contrary tendencies affecting the position of women. On the one hand, the split between home and workplace that became general by the latter stages of the nineteenth century helped foster an association between women and domesticity. Again this seems to have been an ideology which was first nurtured in the higher echelons of the class system, filtering down to other classes. The idea that 'the place of the woman is in the home' had different implications for women at varying levels in society. The more affluent enjoyed the services of maids, nurses, and domestic servants. For those in the middle orders the consequence was that the tasks of women became the domestic duties of caring for home and children, where these were no longer recognised as 'work', at least in a sense parallel to paid employment in production. But the burdens were harshest for a proportion of women in working-class families, having to cope with most of the household chores in addition to engaging in industrial labour. Women who 'worked' – that is, were employed for a gainful wage – in the nineteenth and early twentieth centuries came preponderantly from peasant or working classes (see Louise A. Tilly and Joan W. Scott, *Women, Work and Family*, New York, Holt, Rinehart & Winston, 1978). Drawing upon material from Britain and France, Tilly and Scott conclude that rates of employment of women in manufacturing industry were fairly low, except in textile production. Even as late as 1911 in Britain the majority of working women were employed in domestic or other personal service occupations. More than 33 per cent of gainfully employed women were servants; 16 per cent were engaged in garment-making, many of whom worked at home; some 20 per cent worked in the textile industry. A rather similar pattern of female employment existed in France.

These statistics demonstrate rather clearly that the employment opportunities for women during the period of expansion of industrial capitalism were concentrated in sectors close to traditional tasks which women had carried out. Work in these sectors was, in fact, almost exclusively monopolised by women, with wage-levels considerably below those of male manual workers. The large majority of women workers, however, were young and single. In Britain in 1911, nearly 70 per cent of all single women were employed, but only some 10 per cent of married women were. Since that date, employment patterns of women have changed considerably, following the virtual disappearance of full-time domestic servants and the relative contraction of the textile industry. The most significant change has been connected with a phenomenon noted in a previous chapter: the relative expansion of white-collar occupations in the advanced capitalist countries. The growth of such occupations has coincided with an increasing recruitment of women to office work and to service jobs. But this cannot be interpreted as involving a significant move towards greater sexual equality within the productive system. For women workers are overwhelmingly to be found in work settings of a routinised kind, at the bottom of the hierarchy of authority in office or shop, and with few of the career opportunities open to men. The fate of the occupation of 'clerk' provides a good illustration of how this phenomenon has developed (see pp. 72–3, above). In Britain at the mid-point of the nineteenth century fewer than 1 per cent of clerks were women. But to be a 'clerk', as I have said, was to have a responsible position, involving the use of actuarial and other skills. The twentieth century has seen the general mechanisation of office work, beginning with the introduction of the typewriter in the late nineteenth century, accompanied by the transmutation of the occupation of 'clerical worker' into a series of semi-skilled operations. Today most clerks are women, as are most shop assistants.

Over the period since the Second World War, the proportion of women in the labour force has grown considerably in all the Western countries. The largest increase has been in the percentage of married women working. But although some new career prospects have been opened up for women in occupations that have previously been almost entirely the preserve of men, these are nowhere widespread. A general indication of how poorly women fare in relation to men is offered by comparing the average earnings of female with those of male workers in the labour force. Table 6.1 provides such a calculation for the United States for selected years between 1961 and 1972.

Such figures show that the earnings gap between men and women is, at best, not improving. They are not unrepresentative of the capitalist societies as a whole. Those societies in which official state policy has been more favourable to the incorporation of women into the labour force than in the United States, such as the Scandinavian countries, do not seem markedly superior in respect of the relative level of women's earnings compared with those of men. Participation in the labour force, of course, is only one aspect of the patriarchal relations that tend to prevail in the contemporary capitalist societies. Women are everywhere underrepresented in positions of power in politics and other spheres. Moreover, they are subject to a 'double discrimination' in so far as many working women continue to be primarily responsible for household duties and child care.

Women's rights movements have sought to combat these inequalities in various ways, although most feminist writers have conceded that they are very deeply entrenched. The very pervasiveness of patriarchy in

TABLE 6.1 *Earnings of full-time workers by sex in the United States*

	Median income		Women's earnings as % of men's
	Women	Men	
1961	$3,351	$5,644	59.4
1965	3,823	6,375	60.0
1969	4,977	8,227	60.5
1972	5,903	10,202	57.9
1982	12,001	20,260	59.2

Sources: Barbara M. Wertheimer, 'Search for a partnership role', in Jane Roberts Chapman (ed.) *Economic Independence of Women* London, Sage, 1976, p. 188; *Statistical Abstract of the United States*, 1984.

human societies itself demonstrates this; patriarchy was not brought into the world by the advent of capitalism. However, it is clear enough that the development of capitalism, intertwined with changes in family forms described earlier, is associated with specific modes of sexual domination. There are evident points of connection between gender divisions and the class system. The concentration of working women in relatively poorly paid occupations, having inferior conditions of work and promotion prospects, is influenced by the attitudes of employers and male workers, and by the breaks in women's careers resulting from childbirth. Women continue in some substantial degree to acquiesce in these circumstances, resignedly or otherwise, themselves accepting the 'ideology of domesticity' – placing marriage and the family above the economic rewards that might be derived from full and equal participation in the system of industrial labour. The points at issue here are complex, and feminist writers have tended to be divided about them. The achievement of full sexual equality within work outside the home is not necessarily a desirable end in itself in the context of a capitalist economy. But the transformation or humanisation of capitalist-industrial labour, conversely, would not guarantee the overcoming of sexual exploitation, in so far as this is rooted in the family.

The Family, Marriage, Sexuality

Many sociologists writing about the family have supposed that the development of capitalism has been associated with a radical decline in family size. Generalising – mistakenly – from the large families found in those countries in the Third World that are the main source of the current explosion in world population, they have presented a picture of homes teeming with children in the pre-capitalist period in Europe. Very large families were not uncommon, but they were by no means the norm. Historians working upon seventeenth-century Britain and France have shown that the average age of marriage of females was probably between twenty-three and twenty-seven. The time during which the wife could bear children was limited by this, and by the early age of menopause; but also by the likely occurrence of the premature death of one of the marital partners, and by the very high rates of infant mortality and death of children. The wealthy typically had larger families than the peasants or artisans: age of wives at marriage was lower, and men would remarry more rapidly upon the death of a wife.

The ubiquity and visibility of death is one of the phenomena that most strikingly distinguishes the pre-modern family, and day-to-day social life in general, from the contemporary era. Death rates were several times higher than they are today, and death was not something that happened mainly to the aged. Those living in towns were particularly vulnerable, because of lack of sanitation and the impurity of water supplies – leading to the chronic possibility of epidemic disease. The towns, in fact, did not reproduce themselves, depending for their continuation upon regular migration from the rural areas. Life expectation, as I mentioned in the first chapter of the book, was very low. Probably about a third of infants died within the first year of life; among the peasantry in France in the seventeenth century, on average half died before the age of ten. Neither did young adults escape, having far higher mortality rates than comparable age-groups today. As a consequence, family size among those in the lower classes was probably at any one point in time only around two or three children, although the number of children procreated was very much larger. Half the total population was under twenty, and only a tiny minority over sixty.

The so-called 'demographic transition', which occurred in the eighteenth and nineteenth centuries, was not so much a move from large to small families, as an alteration in the composition of the family in relation to the generations. The 'demographic transition' represented a change from the circumstances just described, occurring principally through a sharp drop in mortality rates of the younger age-groups. Average age of marriage fell, and continued to fall well into this century. The expansion of population which occurred in the nineteenth century was not the result of more children being born, but of more surviving, and surviving longer. The changes described previously, affecting both the nature of the family and the relative position of men and women in the labour force, led to circumstances in which large families were a handicap for those in the working class. In traditional forms of production, where children contributed to economic activity, large families were often actively desired, however much the factors indicated might have limited family size in actuality. But where children do not work, and where many women do not receive paid wages, large families become an economic burden. Improved methods of contraception provided the means of making longer-lasting marriages, centred upon 'affective individualism', compatible with small families – the essential pattern that persists today. This also, of course, has considerable implications for women, for most now have the prospect of a period of some twenty to thirty years' life following the maturity and departure of their children from the home.

Controversies over the current status of marriage and

the family, among sociologists as well as in the lay press, especially in respect of the dissolution of marriages and sexual behaviour, have frequently lacked an adequate historical dimension. The dissolution of marriages was very common in Europe in previous centuries, although as a consequence of death rather than divorce. Some commentators have argued that the relative proportion of children affected by 'broken marriages' was at least as high in the past as it is today. In some countries, and in some periods, in relatively recent European history, pre-marital sexual intercourse was usual for both sexes, and no bar to subsequent marriage; illegitimacy rates have also been as high as, or higher than, they are today. Contemporary trends in marriage, the family, and sexuality, of course, occur in a very different context – as I have sought to document throughout this book – but it is obviously important to understand that they are in some respects not as unique as they may appear.

In most Western countries, divorce rates have climbed steeply over the past two or three decades, as Table 6.2 demonstrates for various selected countries. In the quarter of a century from 1950 to 1975, divorce rates rose by 40 per cent in France, at the lower end of the scale, and by 400 per cent in Britain, at the top. All such statistics have to be treated with some reserve. They do not include, for example, those who live together without being married, or married people who separate without the formality of a divorce. None the less, it would be hard to dispute that they indicate the occurrence of significant changes in the family and marriage in the West. There are those who would argue that they express the imminent disintegration of the nuclear family, which, in its successive forms, has been such a long-standing phenomenon. Some, from a conservative standpoint, view this prospect with despondency, as a measure of the decay of a morally responsible society. Others, of quite a contrary outlook, welcome it as indicative of the possibility of developing other social forms, since they view the family as essentially a repressive institution.

TABLE 6.2 *Numbers of marriages, divorces (in thousands), and divorces per 100 marriages, 1950–80*

	1950	1960	1970	1975	1980
France					
Marriages	331	320	394	387	334
Divorces	35	30	40	67	91
Divorces per 100 marriages	11	9	10	17	27
United Kingdom					
Marriages	408	394	471	429	418
Divorces	30	23	62	129	160
Divorces per 100 marriages	7	6	13	30	38
United States					
Marriages	1,675	1,523	2,159	2,127	2,390
Divorces	387	393	708	1,026	1,189
Divorces per 100 marriages	23	26	33	48	50

Sources: Michael Anderson, 'Quantitative indicators of family change', in Anderson, *Sociology of the Family*, Harmondsworth, Penguin, 1980; *United Nations Statistical Yearbook*, 1984.

It seems likely that there will continue to be a range of experimental forms of social relationships diverging from established family institutions. But a more plausible interpretation than that of the coming dissolution of the family would be that contemporary developments represent the very triumph of 'affective individualism' as a guiding principle of domestic life. It needs no great insight to recognise that rising rates of divorce may indicate, not a deep dissatisfaction with the marital state or with the family as such, but an increased determination to make of these rewarding and satisfying relationships. If divorce rates have risen to previously unheard-of levels, they have been accompanied by very high rates of remarriage. The vast majority of those who divorce remarry. I do not think it would be justifiable, however, to see this phenomenon, as those referred to at the opening of the chapter have tended to do, simply as showing that the family provides an indispensable source of emotional satisfaction for the majority of people in the contemporary societies. The reality is assuredly more complex. Domestic life stands at the intersection of various currents of social change, which it reflects and to which it contributes. Here it is rather important to relate discussion of the family to the concerns of previous chapters. In circumstances in which the mass of the population work in conditions of labour that are dull and oppressive, and in which the commodification of social relations has created a series of empty routines in everyday life, personal relations in the domestic sphere may indeed appear as a refuge from a 'heartless world'. But, in the absence of quite profound transformations in the broader society, the family is likely to remain riven by opposing tensions – liberation and oppression, hope and despair.

The rise of 'affective individualism' has been closely involved with the association of sexuality with personal fulfilment, inside and outside the formal ties of marriage. Some radical writers have argued that the origins and continuation of capitalism are closely bound up psychologically with the repression of sexuality. The strict discipline demanded by industrial labour, in their view, is secured through the generalised curtailing of personal desires, epitomised by Victorian mores in the heyday of nineteenth-century capitalism. According to this standpoint, which in one version or another was widely adopted by those involved in the student movements of the late 1960s, the liberation of sexuality is the key to securing a general emancipation from the routinised nature of work

and everyday life in capitalism. The material I have
discussed in this chapter suggests that we should be
sceptical of this sort of stance. 'Affective individualism'
appears to be a more deeply founded trait of contemporary capitalism than the more restricted and transitory
inroads into the expression of sexuality represented by
Victorian prudery. Foucault has recently expanded upon
this in an interesting way (Michel Foucault, *The History
of Sexuality*, vol. 1, London, Allen Lane, 1978). What
we should try to understand, he proposes, is not how
sexual repression originates, but why we are today so
preoccupied with sexuality, making it the focus of the
striving for self-fulfilment. Liberation from sexuality is
what is required, rather than liberation through sexuality.

Family Life and New Social Patterns

Evidence indicates that, when they first marry, the vast
majority of individuals – even in countries with the highest
divorce rates – believe they are taking on a life-time
commitment. The facts show otherwise. A significant
proportion of marriages contracted today are only of
short duration. Many of those who believed they were
'marrying for life' find themselves living alone at much
earlier ages than was the case when most 'broken'
marriages derived from the death of one of the partners.
Given the propensity of divorced people to marry again,
at any one time a considerable number of those either
living alone or as parents in one-parent families will be
'between marriages'.

Table 6.3 shows the shifts which have occurred over
the past two decades in the United States in the
distribution of individuals living alone. More people live
alone, both in terms of absolute numbers and relative to

others in the population, than was the case twenty years ago. Whereas in 1960 by far the highest proportion of those living by themselves were in the older age-groups, in recent years this pattern has become much less clear-cut. There has been a sharp rise in the proportion of individuals living alone in the 24–44 years age-bracket.

TABLE 6.3 *Persons living alone in the United States*

Sex and age	Number of persons (in thousands)			Percent		
	1960	1975	1982	1960	1975	1982
Both sexes	7,064	13,939	19,354	100	100	100
14–24 years	234	1,111	1,511	3.3	8.0	7.8
25–44 years	1,212	2,744	5,560	17.2	19.7	28.7
45–64 years	2,720	4,076	4,611	38.5	29.2	23.8
65 years and over	2,898	6,008	7,673	41.0	43.1	39.6
Male	2,628	4,918	7,482	37.2	35.3	38.7
14–24 years	124	610	841	1.8	4.4	4.3
25–44 years	686	1,689	3,365	9.7	12.1	17.4
45–64 years	965	1,329	1,784	13.7	9.5	9.2
65 years and over	853	1,290	1,492	12.1	9.3	7.7
Female	4,436	9,021	11,872	62.8	64.7	61.3
14–24 years	110	501	670	1.6	3.6	3.5
25–44 years	526	1,055	2,196	7.4	7.6	11.3
45–64 years	1,755	2,747	2,826	24.8	19.7	14.6
65 years and over	2,045	4,718	6,180	28.9	33.8	31.9

Source: *Statistical Abstract of the United States, 1984.*

The ratio of single to married householders has risen in more or less parallel fashion, as has the proportion of children living with a single parent as compared to married couples. The US census now includes a category of 'unmarried couples sharing the same household'. Since this is something of an innovation, it is not easy to make comparisons with earlier periods. But it certainly is the case among younger age groups that the proportion of unmarried people living together on a regular basis has risen substantially – although the numbers are small compared with the vast army of the married.

Notwithstanding the considerable number of individuals living alone and as one-parent families, plus other forms of household, it remains true that most people live in an 'orthodox' family setting for most of their lives. That is to say, they are members of family units involving a heterosexual married couple, living together with children in one household.

For large number of people however, this is liable to involve two main types of change from the forms of family life with which their parents were familiar. One is that over the course of their lifetime – both as children, and later themselves as parents – they may deviate from the 'orthodox' pattern on several occasions of varying duration. That is to say, during their childhood and adolescence they may live first of all within a family consisting of their parents and siblings. Less commonly they may be born into a family in which only one of a married couple is their biological parent; where both or one of an unmarried cohabiting couple is their biological parent; where neither of the members of a married couple is such a parent (adoption); or into a single-parent household.

The second factor is the increasing importance of step-families in the experience of both children and adults. Step-families were common prior to the 'demographic' transition mentioned earlier, as a result of the high rates of mortality. But very many children now grow up in families where one partner is a step-parent, but where regular contact is maintained with the separated or divorced natural parent. Surely some of the most difficult yet important of modern family relationships centre upon this circumstance. Today's children are, in turn, likely themselves to become both biological parents and step-parents at subsequent phases of their lives. The United States is not far from a situation where living in a step-family will become the predominant form of family life.

The family is simultaneously the focus of profound social change, yet saturated with values deriving from pre-established modes of family organisation. The term 'step-parent' – like the associated terminology of 'broken marriage' or 'broken home' – still has to be wrenched free from the very negative connotations with which it has previously been linked. But in the meantime step-parenting is likely to focus in a particularly acute way the dilemmas and tensions of modern family life.

7

Capitalism and the World System

In the light of the ideas I have set out in earlier pages, it should not appear odd to move directly from the intimacies of domestic life to developments that span the globe. Nothing is more characteristic of our era than the connections between the conduct of our day-to-day lives, specific to time and place, and events in far-flung regions. It is difficult for us, living in a world of more or less instantaneous electronic communication via telephone, radio, and television, and extremely rapid travel by road, rail, and air, to understand the slow pace of communication and travel in previous centuries. In common with so many of the phenomena analysed in this book, this conquest of time and space dates from only the mid-eighteenth century. In the early period of the eighteenth century in Europe, transportation – simultaneously the only means of communication – was almost as slow as it had always been in prior phases of world history, even in empires having developed road systems. Napoleon took almost as long as Caesar had done to get from Rome to Paris. Communication became separated from transportation only with the first successful utilisation of Morse's electromagnetic telegraph between Baltimore and Washington, D.C., in 1844. Morse transmitted the message 'What hath God wrought?' and thereby initiated a new epoch in the transmission of information.

Prior to this, communication over distance was dependent upon human spatial mobility, which was inordinately slow by modern standards. It has been estimated that nearly three-quarters of the population of the United States heard of the assassination of John F. Kennedy within half an hour of the occurrence of the event. About a century and a half before, when George Washington died in Alexandria, Virginia, the news was first published in New York City only seven days later (see Allan R. Pred, *Urban Growth and the Circulation of Information*, Cambridge, Mass., Harvard University Press, 1973). Of course, spatial mobility has also increased enormously since that date. Geographers have introduced the concept of 'time-space convergence' as a simple mode of analysing this. The rate at which two cities are converging in time-space can be calculated by comparing, for example, the length of an average journey made by stage-coach between Edinburgh and London in 1780 with the same journey made by plane in 1980. By such a calculation, the two cities have converged by a factor of 2,000 per cent. The rate of time-space convergence between, say, Tokyo and London would be much higher.

These phenomena are as important for what they indicate as for their substance: that we live in a world in which the majority of the population are interdependent in ways unprecedented in former times. There is today a 'world system', which it will be my object in this chapter to investigate.

Modernisation Theory and its Critique

In Chapter 2, I mentioned that the theory of industrial

society has been closely bound up with a particular view of the relation between the 'developed' (industrialised) societies and the rest of the world – a particular view of the dynamics of the contemporary world system. This approach is often referred to as 'modernisation' theory. Modernisation theory relates to the theory of industrial society in a rather direct way, because its proponents presume that the sort of analysis offered by Dahrendorf and others is basically correct. That is to say, it is assumed that industrialism is essentially a liberalising force and a progressive one; and hence that the Western societies provide a model for 'underdeveloped' societies to follow. Two further consequences follow from this position. First, the traditional societies of the Third World are not just *under*developed, they are *un*developed: they await the impact of industrial transformation. Second, these societies therefore have to tread similar paths to those already followed by the industrialised countries, reproducing the achievements of 'industrial society'.

Modernisation theory continues to be influential in academic circles, although it no longer enjoys the widespread endorsement which it once did, having been subjected to very substantial criticism. But it is important to recognise that from the 1960s to the present day, this type of theory has become an important contributing element to the world system itself. This is because the assumptions upon which it is based are, broadly speaking, shared by Western governments in their interaction with the Third World, and by development agencies associated with the United Nations, the World Bank, and so on. The traits identified as integral to an affluent industrial order are regarded as 'indicators' of development, and have been used to guide political and economic policy towards the non industrialised countries (see the so-called 'Brandt Report': Willy Brandt *et al.*, *North–South: a*

Programme for Survival, London, Pan Books, 1980). The result, however, has been to create difficulties that exacerbate trends which, as I shall discuss below, are increasingly dislocating the world economy. For modernisation theory is based upon false premises, and has served in some degree as an ideological defence of the dominance of Western capitalism over the rest of the world.

The theory of industrial society, as I have pointed out in previous chapters, has very definite limitations, a matter which already compromises modernisation theory. But equally important is the notion that industrial capitalism developed separately from the rest of the world: it is this second assumption that has been most strongly and convincingly subject to attack by authors influenced by a Marxist standpoint. There have been, and continue to be, many controversies among Marxist writers themselves about the formation of the world system and its contemporary characteristics. But on certain points they are agreed. One is that the dynamic underlying modern history is what Marx described as the 'restlessly expanding' character of capitalist production. A second (not specifically worked out by Marx himself) is that the 'underdeveloped' societies have from the earliest phases of capitalist development been *involved with* the capitalist societies in systematic relations of exploitation, organised by the latter to their advantage. Wallerstein has expressed this thesis as follows, drawing a fundamental contrast between the modern world system (dating from the sixteenth and seventeenth centuries) and prior phases of world history. In previous times the most encompassing type of social system, he argues, was the agrarian empire (such as that of traditional China, which endured for some two thousand years). Such empires, however successful, never achieved dominion over more than part of the world. The main connections between the 'centres' of such empires – the administrative apparatus of government – and their 'peripheral' areas were sustained by politico-military power. But from the sixteenth century onwards, accelerating particularly during the nineteenth and twentieth centuries, there has come into being a world capitalist economy. In the world capitalist economy, which by the nineteenth century had already become a genuinely global system, the main connections over a broad territorial scale are economic; politico-military power is in the hands of nation-states, each of which has strictly delimited territories of jurisdiction. In Wallerstein's words, 'capitalism as an economic mode is based on the fact that the economic factors operate within an area larger than that which any political society can totally control' (Immanuel Wallerstein, *The Modern World System*, New York, Academic Press, 1974, p. 348).

According to this standpoint, while the driving impetus to the expansion of capitalism is centred in the West – later joined by other economically developed countries, principally Japan – 'underdevelopment' is not a term that has reference to societies untouched by capitalism. The expansion of capitalism *has given rise to 'underdevelopment'*. While Marxist authors, such as Frank (see below, p. 142), played most part in formulating this sort of standpoint, it has today become accepted by others of different persuasions. Modernisation theory is now rarely advocated with the naïveté of two decades ago, and at least in some respects there is substantial accord over the main characteristics of the contemporary world system.

Most analysts are agreed that there have been three broad phases in the formation of the world capitalist economy. The first phase, lasting approximately from the opening of the sixteenth to the late nineteenth century, was that dominated by 'merchant capitalism'. The earlier date was the first period at which Europe achieved a measure of security from external attack, and began a world-wide expansion of trading operations. For hundreds of years since the decline of 'its' empire, the Roman Empire, Europe was more or less chronically menaced by external powers. In 1241, for example, the Mongols had Europe at their mercy, having emerged victors in a decisive strategic battle. They in fact halted their advance, because of the sudden death of the Mongol chief Ögödai, and because they were more interested in holding sway over the East than over the West. But after that time the independence of Europe – the states of which were continually squabbling among themselves – was threatened by the Ottoman Empire. The repulsion of the Turks from the approaches of Vienna in 1683 was a decisive event in world history. Thereafter the economic, and hence military, development of the European countries gave them a degree of security from external threat which lasted until the first decades of the twentieth century, with the emergence of the 'super powers', the United States and the Soviet Union. Internal security at home was the springboard for the expansion of trading operations overseas.

During the lengthy period of merchant capitalism, traders from Europe, backed where necessary with firepower, 'opened up' the African coasts, Asia, and North and South America. They established outposts in all these regions, and initiated the migration from Europe to the Americas that was subsequently to transform these continents totally. In Africa and Asia in the seventeenth and eighteenth centuries the conduct of trade was usually organised by the granting of monopolistic privileges to corporate bodies of merchants – such as the East India Company. These were only superficially purely mercantile organisations: their activities were directly backed by the threat or use of force. Such bodies were thereby able to extract conditions of exchange that frequently amounted to looting sanctioned by state patronage. The result was a vast transfer of wealth to Europe from the rest of the world, this wealth partly being appropriated by the state, partly used as capital to fund investment in manufacture in Europe.

Thus Spain drew massive amounts of silver from Mexico and Peru; Portugal gold from Brazil. England profited from pirating operations against the Spanish and the Portuguese; and subsequently in India and elsewhere was able to enforce terms of trade which ensured a considerable outflow of wealth from colonised regions. The results of these endeavours, of course, depended also upon changes internal to Europe, and thus varied from country to country. Whereas in England the inflow of raw materials, gold, and silver helped fuel an emerging indigenous industry, in Spain and Portugal the influx of wealth tended to lead to the running down of internal economic production.

The 'development of underdevelopment' occurring during the phase of merchant capitalism took place on three connected levels, varying with time and place: the cultural, economic, and political erosion of the societies drawn into the orbit of Western commerce. None of these forms of destructive contact is peculiar to the expansion of Western capitalism, or to the modern era either. Throughout human history, particularly since the origin of 'civilisations', which have virtually everywhere been associated with an escalation of military power, we can read a dismal record of the dissolution, absorption, or wholesale slaughter of some societies by others. What is different about the modern epoch of Western power has been the massive and continuing character of these processes. The destruction of the cultural distinctiveness of other societies has proceeded in some part by the direct imposition of Western modes of life, but has also involved physical extermination on a grand scale. Probably as many as 15 million African slaves were transported to the Americas; however, a high proportion of those who set out died en route, so the actual numbers uprooted from their homelands was far higher. Disease and malnutrition brought about by contact with Europeans further swelled this total. In North America, the indigenous population was all but completely wiped out by the end of the nineteenth century; it has been calculated that the native population of South America was cut by 40 per cent between the early sixteenth century and the middle of the nineteenth century. The economic decline of societies brought within the world capitalist economy has been well documented. Traditional forms of production were undermined through the European demand for cash crops, or establishing trading patterns were broken up. Political dissolution was either attendant upon cultural and economic change, or the result of direct intervention in existing mechanisms of administration.

The idea of the 'development of underdevelopment' was first stated by Frank (André Gunder Frank, *Capitalism and Underdevelopment in Latin America*, Harmondsworth, Penguin, 1971) and, as described by him, has been subject to considerable criticism. Frank regards 'underdevelopment' as deriving from the effect of Western merchant capital in preventing indigenous economic development through its dominance over the latter. Others, while accepting that 'underdevelopment' is a created phenomenon, place more emphasis upon the various forms of political control, and upon the deliberate confinement of industrial production to the West. It is also certainly important to emphasise that the period of merchant capitalism was not wholly one of the despoliation of other parts of the world. Like other 'civilisations' before it, Western capitalism mixed its degradations with genuine benefits: peaceful coexistence was sometimes established between erstwhile warlike neighbours, and the power of exploitative local landlords broken. Something similar is true of the second phase, that of colonialism. The period of colonialism, which has only come to an end over the past two decades or so, significantly redressed one of the major elements involved in the earlier European contacts with other peoples: the introduction of diseases against which those peoples had little or no resistance.

The expansion of European colonialisation from the sixteenth century until the late nineteenth century was the vehicle of successive waves of catastrophic epidemics in the areas involved. Smallpox, measles and typhus were almost certainly unknown in Central and South America prior to the arrival of the Spanish soldiers and traders. These diseases swept through a population having little or no natural immunity to them. A similar fate befell many North American tribal groups as a result of contacts established by the English and the French. The most devastating source of the transmission of deadly diseases was the slave trade, which carried such diseases to unprotected populations from West Africa to the Americas, and vice versa, from the Americas back to Africa.

In the twentieth century, however, schemes of health care based upon modern medicine, particularly via inoculation and improved sanitation, brought about a decline in mortality rates in colonised countries comparable to that witnessed in Europe rather earlier. Some illnesses previously accepted as inevitable – smallpox, tuberculosis, diphtheria, and others – were controlled or virtually eradicated. One of the most fundamental outcomes of this, in the absence of the factors that helped limit birth rates in Europe, has been the enormous expansion of world population.

Colonialism, seen as a 'responsibility' to be shouldered by Western governments, was often initially undertaken only reluctantly. The processes of cultural, economic, and political dissolution described above brought substantial areas in need of direct political administration by the Western powers if they were to maintain their economic advantages. Colonialism engendered a 'dual' system in the colonised societies – a social form which persists today in the settings of post-colonialism. Again, interpretations of the details of dualism vary, but there is a consensus about its general nature. Dualism exists in respect of all three dimensions I have mentioned; in each case it refers to the existence of two sets of institutions within the colonised society, separate from but related to one another. Economic dualism may take various forms, but essentially means that a 'developed', or industrialised, sector coexists with more traditional economic activities in other sectors or regions of the country. This is usually associated with extreme inequalities of wealth and income between the two sectors, and has in many countries produced large-scale migrations from deprived rural areas into cities which do not possess either the economic or administrative means to cope with the migrants. Urban development does not run parallel to industrialisation, as happened in Europe; cities in the Third World tend to have 'modern' – Westernised – centres, and a certain development of commerce and industry, surrounded at their periphery by shanty towns in which most of the population carries on a hand-to-mouth existence. Cultural and political dualism is usually fairly closely connected with economic dualism. The first refers to the fact that traditional modes of life survive alongside the Westernised centres; the second to the establishment of a political apparatus of government staffed by Westernised officials, with the higher administrators supplied by the colonial power. With de-colonisation the result frequently has been a 'top heavy' society, having developed governmental institutions presiding over a country disrupted by the economic deprivations of colonialism (see Peter Worsley, *The Three Worlds. Culture and World Development*, London, Weidenfeld, 1984).

There can be no doubt that the colonial period continued, and accelerated, the 'development of underdevelopment'. Colonial exploitation involved, besides other things, organised modes of economic imbalance between the Western nations and their colonised regions. The Western powers directly established the production and marketing of raw materials in the colonies to promote their own industrial growth, often devoting most of the arable land to the cultivation of one or two particularly profitable cash crops. The native population then found themselves with little productive land to support their own needs. Moreover, whatever benefits might have accrued to the colonised country through its cash crops – most being appropriated by the colonial power – were negated by fluctuations in the world market for those crops. In periods of boom in the sale of rubber, cocoa, coffee, sugar, and other cash crops, profits would flow outside the colonised country; when prices were dropped, that country would have few resources to fall back on, because of the lack of diversification of its products.

The current phase of development of the world economy is that of post-colonialism, all the main areas subject to direct colonial rule having won their independence as 'new nations'. But these countries still experience the burdens of exploitation that are the outcome of the circumstances described above. The huge degree of economic inequality between the 'developed' and what are now usually called 'less developed' (rather than 'underdeveloped') countries can be readily mapped on a world scale by comparing the wealthy 'North' with the relatively impoverished 'South'. Most of the industrialised countries are situated north of the equator, the less developed countries in the equatorial areas or to the south. Thus Africa, Latin America and south India, continents which for the most part are relatively poor, are all located towards the southern areas of the major land masses of the world. The United States, Europe and Japan lie more towards the north.

Contemporary World Inequalities

So far I have talked of the 'First' and 'Third Worlds' without mention of the 'Second World' – that of the socialist countries of the Soviet Union, Eastern Europe, China, Cuba, and elsewhere. The category of 'Second World' in some part cuts across the North–South division. The socialist countries, explicitly affiliated to Marxism, have in some part taken themselves out of the world capitalist economy. In other words, by instituting planned economies based on the suppression or strict limitation of privately owned capital, these countries have extricated themselves in some degree from the exploitative relations that persist between the West and the Third World. We have to say 'in some degree', because the Soviet Union and the Eastern European societies have in fact a considerable number of economic ties with the West; they are therefore by no means wholly insulated from factors influencing Western economic development. Economic recession in the capitalist 'centre' has direct consequences for the socialist countries.

It is quite easy to give a general portrayal of the relative economic standing of the three main sectors in the world system. The 'capitalist' centre occupies about one quarter of world territory, has one-fifth of the total world population, but three-fifths of output. The overall output of the socialist countries is less than half that of the developed capitalist societies of the West and Japan. However, it is still more than twice as high as that of the Third World countries (see Ranjit Sau, *Unequal Exchange, Imperialism and Underdevelopment*, Calcutta, Oxford University Press, 1978).

An indication of the scale of global inequalities is given in Table 7.1. This table concerns the non-socialist sectors of the world Gross Domestic Production.

TABLE 7.1 *Global contrasts in levels of production, 1975 (in per cent of world totals)*

	GDP	Agriculture	Industrial activity	Transport and communications
Developed market economies	81.5	51.2	81.0	84.3
Developing market economies	18.5	48.8	19.0	15.7
Africa, excluding South Africa	3.0	10.7	2.5	2.5
United States and Canada	33.9	15.9	30.6	34.6

Source: *United Nations Statistical Yearbook, 1981.*

GDP (Gross Domestic Product, or total economic output), together with its major sub-divisions, agricultural production, industrial production and transport and communication, are expressed as proportions of all production world-wide. 'Developed market economies' refers to what I have called the capitalist 'centre', or the First World countries, while 'developing market economies' make up the bulk of the Third World countries. The table makes clear how dominant the First World countries are in respect of global production – 81.5 per cent of GDP derives from these countries, with only 18.5 per cent emanating from those in the Third World.

The Continent of Africa, if South Africa is left out of the reckoning, accounts for no more than 3 per cent of total GDP. That of the United States and Canada, by contrast, accounts for fully a third of the total. Similar contrasts appear within the sub-divisions of production. Although they have very small agricultural sectors relative to other areas of production, the First World countries nevertheless control over half the total agricultural production and over 80 per cent of that of manufacturing industry and transport and communications.

The period of de-colonialisation occurring since the Second World War has been accompanied by a very important development in the nature of international capitalism: the increasingly prominent role played by the 'transnational corporations'. In discussing trends within the capitalist economies, I have already referred to the increased centralisation of economic life in the hands of large firms. The growth of these firms internally has generally been built upon a world-wide expansion of the range of their activities and involvements. With the demise of direct colonial rule on the part of the Western states, the transnational corporations have tended to become a leading influence in the world economy, especially as regards their commitments with Third World countries. In a certain sense, of course, this is not a wholly new phenomenon: the great monopoly trading companies of the earlier phases in the development of the world capitalist economy were their precursors. But the post-war growth of transnational capitalism has some quite distinctive features. The transnational corporations are engaged in a far wider range of economic activities across the world than were their predecessors. They have revenues which rival or surpass the GDP of even some of the industrialised countries. Eleven of the twenty-four OECD countries have a GDP smaller than Exxon.

A transnational corporation may be defined as a combination of firms located in different countries, unified by common ownership and hence having a co-ordinated overall strategy. All transnational corporations have 'parent' companies located in specific countries. The United States is easily dominant in this respect, followed by Britain and West Germany (see Robert Gilpin, *U.S. Power and the Multinational Corporation*, London, Macmillan, 1976). Because they are global organisations, the transnational corporations are able to canalise their resources in ways which enable them to circumvent some of the restrictions which states may seek to place upon them. For example, several of the giant automobile manufacturers have integrated their production internationally, enabling them to take advantage of variations in the costs of labour-power and materials across the world. Thus the Ford Escort is a 'world car', standardised in its production globally, in such a way that production arrangements can be fairly readily altered without much regard to national boundaries. Nonetheless, the country in which the parent company is situated is not a trivial matter, for the highest policy decisions tend to be taken in that country, and the flow of profit channelled into it. The national distribution of parent companies thus strongly influences the world pattern of capital accumulation.

The overall consequences of the involvements of the transnational corporations in the Third World have been much debated – as have the implications for the problem of whether the divisions between the rich and poor nations are widening or narrowing. Some have regarded their activities as merely one further step in the exploitation of the less developed countries in favour of the capitalist 'centre'. There is no shortgage of examples of circumstances in which the transnational companies have pursued policies highly detrimental to the poorer countries. Thus, for instance, Western companies have initiated major promotional campaigns in some such countries over the past twenty years, with the aim of converting mothers of infants to the use of dried skim milk and other baby-food products. The consequent spread of bottle-feeding in place of breast-feeding has been shown to be the direct cause of substantial rises in infant mortality. Human milk not only has a lower bacterial level than manufactured milk, but also develops certain short-term anti-infective qualities as well as providing longer-term immunological defences against a range of illnesses.

But the picture is more complicated than such examples may suggest. The transnational corporations invest large capital sums in the countries in which their subsidiaries operate, and increasingly have tended to locate factories in those countries, taking advantage of close access to sources of cheap raw materials and of labour. One result is what has been called 'disarticulation' – a contributing factor to dualism. Disarticulation is where, in Amin's words, the economy is composed 'of sectors, of firms, which are juxtaposed and not highly integrated among themselves, but which are, each on its own, strongly integrated in entities whose centres of gravity lie in the centres of the capitalist world' (S. Amin, *Accumulation on a World Scale*, New York, Monthly Review Press, 1971, p. 289).

Thus a study of the biggest manufacturing firms in Mexico indicated foreign owned firms composed well over forty-five per cent of the total. Similar research in Brazil has yielded very similar conclusions, reinforced by the finding that these large foreign firms also control a very extensive network of smaller companies. At the same time, however, the locating of direct productive capacity in the poorer countries of the world provides at least the potential for them to develop an economic base which could be the foundation for increased material prosperity. Much depends upon the particular situation in the 'host' country: how much control can be achieved over the inflow and outflow of capital, and how far there exists a diversified economic sector outside that dominated by international capital.

The most likely scenario in the coming decades seems to be one in which the majority of Third World countries will remain in circumstances of relative poverty, but where in other respects the economic power of the West will become substantially eroded. In forming an economic cartel (OPEC), the oil-producing countries have been able to emerge as a major power-centre outside the main capitalist core. But this is not a strategy which is likely to be repeated with similar success in respect of other minerals, since oil resources are both more concentrated in certain areas, and of more fundamental importance to the economy of the West than any other raw material. Much more important is the formation of sites of industrial production outside the capitalist 'centre', able to compete effectively with Western products. This seems to be initiating what appears likely to be a continuing trend towards the 'de-industrialisation' of the West, in which Western manufacturing industries suffer a decline or become undermined altogether. Partly as a result of the activities of the transnational corporations, and partly due to indigenous enterpreneurial expansion, countries such as Brazil and Venezuela in Latin America, and South Korea, Hong Kong, and Taiwan, have been able successfully to challenge the Capitalist 'centre' on its own ground. If the tendency towards the relocation of manufacturing industry from core to periphery continues, the consequences for the West may be far-reaching. 'Stagflation' – low growth rates associated with high inflation – may become a normal phenomenon in the West, coupled with rates of unemployment previously regarded as specific to the Third World.

The Nation-State, Nationalism, Military Power

In approaching the topics of the nation-state, nationalism, and military power, we have to depart from drawing contrasts between the theory of industrial society and Marxist theories. For neither tradition of thought has produced anything like adequate interpretations of these phenomena. That this should be so seems, on the face of it, quite extraordinary. For the period of the emergence of a 'world capitalist economy', over the past three centuries or so, has also been one in which the nation-state has become the prevailing form of political unity the world over. The expansion of capitalism has from the sixteenth century onwards been closely integrated with the military power – especially sea-power – of the West. Nationalism has come to be one of the foremost influences in the contemporary world, associated with movements ranging from fascism to left-wing radicalism. Warfare and violence have achieved a hitherto unparalleled escalation in the twentieth century, which has witnessed two world wars and the concentrated destruction of millions of people in other wars. And yet these horrors usually go unmentioned in sociology, whatever the varying persuasions of authors in other respects.

How could such a situation have arisen? One reason

that might be offered is the academic differentiation of 'sociology' from 'political science', mentioned in Chapter 4, the analysis of the state being regarded as the prerogative of the second of these. But the fact is that, even as worked out under this category, the analysis of the state has been heavily deficient, being concerned above all with the internal constitution of democracy, or with the state's economic role. The literature on the 'development of underdevelopment', which I have discussed in the previous section, is of considerable importance in seeking to understand the formation of the modern world system. But for the most part it is written almost wholly on an economic level, as if the sole significant influences in the world system were the production and exchange of goods. An explanation of how these emphases have come to predominate has to look back to the intellectual legacy bequeathed to sociology from the late eighteenth and the nineteenth centuries. Both the theory of industrial society and Marxism were strongly conditioned by the idea that the development of modern industry substitutes peaceful economic exchange relations for the militaristic order of feudalism. The main forms of conflict are economic, and in each case are due to be transcended – in the first instance by the maturation of industrialism as such, in the second via a process of socialist revolution. In neither tradition of thought is the modern state perceived to be linked in an integral way with the propagation of military violence, or with the administrative control of a delimited territorial area. The state, in short, is not conceived of as a nation-state, existing in relations of potential or actual antagonism towards other nation-states. Marx also specifically failed to anticipate the enormous impact that ideals of nationalism have had throughout the contemporary era; ironically enough, nationalistic sentiments have played an important role in stimulating some of the major twentieth-century revolutions installing Marxist governments.

To understand the rise of the modern nation-state, we have to connect the origins of capitalism to the pre-existing social conditions of post-mediaeval Europe. Europe in the sixteenth century was a network of small states – a state system involving shifting alignments, alliances, and conflicts. Whether or not it was a necessary condition for the emergence of capitalism, the existence of the state system was the backcloth to its expansion. These were not yet nation-states. The nation-state can be defined as comprising institutions of political governance where a society's rulers successfully monopolise control of the means of violence (the army and police), that control being the chief sanction backing their administration of a precisely bounded territorial area. The European states in the sixteenth century were not nation-states in this sense; for the most part they had relatively fluid boundaries, and lacked the centralised state apparatus which subsequently gradually came into being. The transformations in transportation and communication I referred to at the beginning of the chapter played an essential part in the process, and were at the same time bound up with the forms of urban development described earlier. These made possible a degree of co-ordination of governmental administration which could not be achieved previously. At the same time, the expansion of industrial production, when connected to the arts of war, afforded an unprecedented build-up of military power. The early European state system was thus the foundation upon which nation-states were later consolidated. Warfare and diplomacy shaped these changes. In the sixteenth century, there were some 500 more or less autonomous states and principalities in Europe; by the turn of the twentieth century these had shrunk to twenty-five (see Charles Tilly, *The Formation of National States in Europe*, Princeton, Princeton University Press, 1975).

The formation of modern nation-states was closely related to the rise of nationalist sentiments. Nationalism can be defined as shared feelings of attachment to symbols which identify the members of a given population as belonging to the same overall community. The development of nationalism in Europe was more or less convergent with the formation of nation-states. It is therefore a quite recent phenomenon, more sharply defined than the diffuse feelings of communality found in earlier phases of development of the European state system. It seems clear that the sharpening of nationalist feelings in Europe was related to the destruction of local community ties, affiliations, dialects, and so on, by the processes of centralisation involved in the advent of the nation-state. None the less, it is also evident that the nation-state and nationalism should not be thought of as merely two sides of the same coin. The post-colonial states in contemporary Africa, for example, are certainly nation-states, but some are beset by regional divisions stronger than sentiments of attachment to the national community.

If the capitalist world economy is a distinctive feature of the modern world system, so then also is the nation-state system. Wallerstein points this out, but does not seem to pursue the implications of the observation fully enough. For the global diffusion of the nation-state has been accompanied by an ever-increasing accumulation of the means of waging war in the hands of nation-states. Amin's phrase 'accumulation on a world scale' applies to the development of armaments as much as to the growth of material wealth as such – culminating in the current era of the spread of nuclear weapons, an era which leaves us all on a knife-edge of survival.

Conclusion: Sociology as Critical Theory

In this book I have sought to introduce the reader to a conception of sociology at variance with modes of thinking which have for a long period been dominant in the subject. Those who have wanted to model sociology upon natural science, hoping to discover universal laws of social conduct, have tended to sever sociology from history. In breaking with such views, we have to go further than simply asserting that sociology and history – or, more accurately, the social sciences and history – are indistinguishable, provocative though such a claim may appear to be. We have to grasp how history is made through the active involvements and struggles of human beings, and yet at the same time both forms those human beings and produces outcomes which they neither intend nor foresee. As a theoretical background to the social sciences, nothing is more vital in an era suspending between extraordinary opportunity on the one hand and global catastrophe on the other.

Abandoning the orthodox view also means rejecting the notion that sociology can be restricted to description and explanation. Sociology, together with the social sciences in general, is inherently and inescapably part of the 'subject-matter' it seeks to comprehend. As a critical enterprise, sociological thought has to be structured around the three dimensions of the sociological imagination which I distinguished. In gaining some comprehension of forms of society that have faded into the past, and of others whose ways of life are radically discrepant from those fostered by current processes of social change, we can help fulfil the tasks of sociology as critical theory. As critical theory, sociology does not take the social world as a given, but poses the questions: what types of social change are feasible and desirable, and how should we strive to achieve them?

There are some who would claim that Marxism offers ready-made solutions to these issues, and who would therefore simply seek to substitute 'Marxism' for 'sociology'. This is not my view, for two reasons. One is that there is not the dichotomy between Marxism and sociology which this standpoint presupposes. Sociological thought should be prepared to absorb contributions emanating from the Marxist tradition without becoming dissolved into it. My second reason supplies the logic for this view: there are too many flaws and inadequacies in Marxist thought for it to supply an overall grounding for sociological analysis.

Marx's writings are of essential importance to sociology in respects which I have tried to indicate in discussing the contrasts between Marxist thought and the theory of industrial society. The expansion of capitalistic enterprise gave the impetus to the subsequent development of industrial production in the West. The Western societies remain capitalistic in character, however much they may have changed since the period at which Marx wrote. Class struggle has both been directly involved with these changes, and continues to be central both to industrial relations and to the nature of the state. The dynamic character of capitalist production gives rise to rates of technological innovation vastly greater than anything known in any preceding type of production system. Marx was not guilty of understatement when he wrote that 'It [capitalist enterprise] has accomplished wonders far surpassing Egyptian pyramids, Roman aqueducts, and Gothic cathedrals; it has conducted expeditions that put in the shade all former Exoduses of nations and crusades . . . Constant revolutionising of production, uninterrupted disturbance of all social conditions, everlasting uncertainty and agitation distinguish the bourgeois epoch from earlier ones.' Moreover, as Marx frequently emphasised, this dynamism spreads capitalistic economic mechanisms across the globe: capitalist industries 'no longer work up indigenous raw material, but raw material drawn from the remotest zones; industries whose products are consumed, not only at home, but in every quarter of the globe' (Karl Marx and Friedrich Engels, 'Manifesto of the Communist Party', in *Selected Works in One Volume*, London, Lawrence & Wishart, 1968, pp. 38 and 39).

Marxist thought has developed in a rich and diverse way since the time at which Marx wrote. Marxism, in one form or another, has also of course become the official idea-system followed by governments holding sway over very substantial sectors of the world. But at the very time of its political success, its limitations as a body of theory and practice have become increasingly apparent. Socialist revolutions, as everyone knows, have taken place in countries on the periphery of capitalism, rather than in the industrially advanced heartlands of the West. The significance of this for the assessment of socialist programmes as a whole continues to be a matter of fierce debate. For it is difficult to deny that the Soviet Union and the other socialist countries, while varying considerably among themselves, seem at best rather distant from the humane and free social order that is the socialist ideal. The specific circumstances in which the

Soviet Union developed, as a society undergoing very rapid industrialisation in an environment surrounded by hostile capitalist powers, undoubtedly served to create some of the authoritarian features that it has come to display. The influence of the Soviet Union over subsequently formed socialist societies has helped to reproduce similar elements there. It is possible to generate penetrating Marxist critiques of Soviet-type societies, and indeed a goodly number have appeared in recent years – mostly, although not exclusively, penned by Marxists living in the West. But it remains a fundamental problem how far some of the totalitarian characteristics of the existing socialist societies are to be traced to limitations in Marx's ideas at source. If such is the case, as I think it to be, contemporary political theory stands in need of a more profound reconstruction than is possible for those who fear to stray too far from the confines of Marx's own doctrines.

Most of Marx's critics are of conservative or liberal political persuasion. But I think it important for a critical social theory, while drawing upon the work of such authors, to outflank Marx from the Left. In addition to the basic issue of the origins of totalitarian political control, there seem to me to be four further sets of questions linked to human emancipation which are inadequately analysed both in Marx's texts and in the writings of most subsequent Marxists (I have not had the space to discuss all of these in this book).

First. The question of the relation of human beings to nature, and the resources which it offers to sustain human life. While Marx does occasionally make a few intriguing and suggestive comments about nature, the main tendency of his work is to treat nature simply as a medium of human social progress. Social advancement, in other words, is identified with the development of industry, of what Marx calls the 'forces of production'. Marx thought of capitalism as a progressive mode of production, whatever the disparities to which it may give rise, precisely because it erodes other – more economically stagnant – social forms.

But to subordinate other modes of relating to nature to the quest for material prosperity may be to destroy ways of life from which the West could have a great deal to learn. For nature, it could be said, for most other cultures prior to the emergence of Western capitalism, is far more than the simple medium of material progress. Human beings do not live, as they have learned to do in modern urban environments, at a distance from nature. For us the 'countryside' (that which has been left unravaged by industry or not made uniform by commercial farming) is an object of contemplation, somewhere to escape to at weekends. However, in most cultures, and for virtually the whole of human history, human beings have lived 'in' nature, feeling themselves to be part of it, intermingling aesthetic and religious experience. We only occasionally catch a glimpse of the depth of such experience, in a fragmentary and residual way. T. S. Eliot suggests something of this in *Burnt Norton*, when he writes of the elusive but elegiac mood induced by 'the moment in the rose-garden, the moment in the arbour where the rain beat, the moment in the draughty church at smokefall . . .'

Should we presume that such instants are all that can, or should, survive in the modern world? If so, we write off thousands of years of human history, and the modes of life of a multiplicity of human societies, as no more than archaic curiosities. Even supposing we did adopt such a view, which today, by a curious reversal, itself seems positively barbaric, it has become clear in the twentieth century that there are ecological limits to the utilisation of nature by human industry. The contemporary stress upon economic development, common to both the capitalist and socialist societies, is tilting the world towards ecological disaster. Whilst a redistribution of productive wealth in the direction of the Third World nations is a matter of urgency, it is of the first importance to resist the conception that the economic problems confronting the world today can be resolved merely through yet more technological innovation. One form of radicalism, then, needed to complement the traditional concerns of Marxism is an ecological radicalism, which seeks to combat a purely instrumental attitude to nature.

Second. The problem of racial or ethnic oppression. Marx's writings, and those of subsequent Marxists, have certainly illuminated aspects of these phenomena in so far as they have played a role in the expansion of capitalism. Since the early days of the slave trade, peoples from the Third World have been more or less forcibly 'imported', or attracted by the promise of higher living standards, into the metropolitan capitalist countries. One of the latest of such developments has been the widespread employment of immigrant workers from poorer countries in the affluent societies of Western Europe. An example is the importation of Turkish 'guest workers' into West Germany in the 1950s and 1960s. Such workers – where they have not returned home – have become clustered in occupations having low wages, little chance of career advancement, and lacking job security.

Ethnic oppression in the advanced capitalist societies cannot be understood except in the context of the history of Western colonialism, and the attitudes which underlay it. Such attitudes have a tenacious quality to them, as the fate of blacks and other 'non-white' minorities in the United States demonstrates. There are clear and systematic differences between the experience of such groups and that of the white immigrants who came in great waves from Europe in the nineteenth and early twentieth centuries. Many of the latter were themselves fleeing from oppressive conditions in the lands of their origin, and found themselves living in circumstances of considerable poverty in the nation to which they came. But for most – but by no means all – of their descendants, the United States has proved to be a 'melting pot', whereby they have become assimilated with the host society. The 'non-white' minorities, on the other hand, have evidently not been assimilated in the same way as the European migrants. Poor employment conditions and segregation in urban ghettos have become apparently permanent features of their conditions of life (see Robert Blauner, *Racial Oppression in America*, New York, Harper & Row, 1972).

But ethnic oppression has by no means been specific to capitalism, and it follows that the transformation of capitalism will not in and of itself put an end to it. The existing socialist societies are certainly not free from ethnic discrimination. We should not see this as surprising, for, in whatever version it might be applied, Marxist thought lacks a treatment of such discrimination as an independent source of exploitation – independent, that is, of mechanisms of class domination. For although ethnic oppression has become closely tied to class divisions in contemporary capitalism, it would be an error to reduce the one to the other. One of the objectives of a critical social theory has to be to produce analyses of ethnic discrimination and exploitation that will escape the traditional preoccupation of Marxist thought with class domination.

Third. The issue of sexual oppression. The questions to be posed here have a similarity to those arising in the case of ethnic divisions. Marxist writers have contributed a good deal to the study of the oppression of women in relation to the rise of capitalism. I have discussed some such work earlier. In separating home from workplace, the development of capitalism, in conjunction with specific features of family life, fostered ideals of domesticity which drastically influenced the position of women in society. Like ethnic minorities – and in heightened degree in the case of women who are also members of such minorities – paid female labour tends to be concentrated in inferior work conditions. All this having been said, Marxist thought, unless substantially reconstructed, cannot cope adequately with the origins and nature of sexual exploitation.

Marx himself wrote little on the matter. His friend and close associate Friedrich Engels, however, did attempt a systematic account of the subjugation of women in his *The Origin of the Family, Private Property and the State* (1884). We cannot say how far Marx agreed with the details of Engels's analysis, but there seems no reason to suggest that he would have disputed the general themes of Engles's view. Following the work of certain nineteenth-century anthropologists, Engels argued that the earliest forms of human society are matriarchal – women are dominant. Male dominance, and patriarchal family institutions, are the product of history. The development of patriarchy is associated with the emergence of classes and the state. Patriarchy has its beginnings in the need of men to protect newly acquired propertied interests (although it must be remarked that Engels does not explain very clearly how this came about). In Engels's theory, therefore, male dominance is explained directly in terms of class. Since patriarchy is an outcome of class domination, it will disappear, Engels reasons, with the transcendence of capitalism by socialism – by the arrival of the classless society.

Not much of Engles's account has retained its validity

in the light of the findings of the social sciences since his day. Anthropological evidence indicates that no matriarchal stage has existed in the development of society. As I have mentioned in Chapter 6, all known cultures are patriarchal in definite aspects – including, it should be pointed out, the existing socialist societies – although there is a considerable variation across the range of different social systems. Patriarchy cannot be 'explained away' as an expression of class domination; like ethnic oppression, it needs to be analysed in its own terms, and practical programmes of social change concerned with women's liberation are not likely to get very far if this is not acknowledged. Feminism may well be more radical in its implications for social life than Marxism.

Fourth. The problem of state power, including its association with the propagation of violence. The prominence accorded to class domination in Marxist theory, as I have tried to show earlier in this text, leads to a double failure in this context. Since, in pre-capitalist as well as in capitalist societies, the state is interpreted solely as the medium of sustaining the rule of the dominant class, there is no room for recognising it as an independent source of power. Partly as a result of this emphasis, Marxism lacks an account of the modern nation-state, and of the world state system, in relation to military power.

The ramifications of these points are complicated, but one could hardly overestimate their significance. So far as the internal constitution of the modern state is concerned, they bear directly upon the need for a theory of totalitarianism. Marx anticipated the transcendence of the state in a socialist society, but for reasons I have tried to make clear in the preceding chapter, the state has turned out to be a far more formidable phenomenon than it is conceived to be in Marxist thought. No great sociological sophistication is required to see that, far from disappearing in the socialist societies, the state has a greater range of powers over the individual citizen in those societies than in the capitalist liberal democracies: they are *state socialist* societies. The specific circumstances shaping the development of the Soviet Union, and its influence over subsequent socialist movements, are certainly relevant to explaining how such has come to be the case. But it would be short-sighted indeed to suppose that this is all there is to the matter.

Important as these 'internal' political questions are, they pale into insignificance when compared with those concerned with the nation-state and violence. One of the main elements of Marx's critique of capitalism was directed against what he called the 'anarchy' of capitalist production. The driving impetus of capitalist enterprise is the pursuit of profit, through the sale of goods on the market. Market mechanisms relate producer and consumer; there is no directive agency which connects production to human needs. This remains the case in modern economic relations, save that some of these 'anarchic' elements are located in the world economy rather than within the economies of particular countries. However, there is now another 'anarchy', which threatens the very survival of everyone on this planet: that of the relations among nation-states. The world nation-state system, in which there is now located control of weapons of unparalleled destructive potential, lacks any overall co-ordinating political apparatus. Those who claim that the era of the nation-state is over, because of the advent of international communities such as the EEC, or because of the existence of agencies such as the United Nations, the World Bank, the International Monetary Fund, and so on, are talking pure nonsense. The two 'super powers', which hold it within their capacity to destroy the world, are nation-states, as are the other nuclear powers – whose numbers expand year by year. Socialism, at least in the forms which it has assumed so far, has not helped to lead towards a peaceful commonwealth of nations. In the shape of the Soviet Union, it is locked into the very heart of the antagonisms that threaten the world's future; and as the embittered relations between the Soviet Union and China, or between Vietnam and its socialist neighbours show, the contemporary socialist state is a nation-state, no different from other nation-states in terms of a jealous territoriality and proclivity to employ military violence when its rulers perceive their interests to be menaced.

A radical social theory must attempt to attain a more adequate understanding of the world nation-state system than is possible for those working within an unreconstructed Marxist tradition; and its main practical concern has surely to be with the support of social movements which seek to contain, and eventually dissolve altogether, the current reliance upon 'deterrence' as the only means of coping with 'anarchy' in the nation-state system. At this juncture of world history, we seem far removed indeed from the scenario which Marx sketched out somewhere near the mid-point of the nineteenth century. Marx had confidence in the progressive development of humankind, summed up in his famous statement that 'human beings only set themselves such tasks as they can resolve'. Surely we can no longer share that confidence; but neither need we lapse into resigned despair. For human beings *do* make their own history, and we can still retain the hope that an understanding of that history will allow us to change it – or at the very least will permit us to ensure that it is a continuing one . . .

Index

power – *continued*
  military, and conflict 80, 139,
    140–2, 152–5
  negative, of workers 64, 86
  political, of capitalist class 36
  state 100, 164–5
  over work processes, loss of
    82
  of working class 64, 77, 85–6
pre-capitalist 15, 16, 21
  everyday life 112–13
  and modern cities, compared
    92–4, 98–100
Pred, A. R. 136
prediction and control 10, 12
prisons 113–14
privacy, restricted 119
private
  rented housing 105, 106, 110
  see also ownership
production
  expropriation of means of 35
  levels, global contrasts 64,
    147–52
  for profit 56
  specialised 16
profit, production for 56
progressive movement,
    industrialisation as 26
proletarianisation of clerical
    work 58, 123
property
  alienability of 101–2
  qualifications for voting rights
    37
  see also ownership
'prose of life' 112–13, 114
protest movements, urban 107–
  8
public *see* state

race
  and housing 106–7
  and oppression 161–2
'rational-legal' norms 80

rebellions, peasant 87–8
recession 63
're-commodification' 79
redistribution of wealth, needed
  161
relationships, patterns of 12
'relative autonomy' of state 74,
  76–7
religion and pre-industrial
    society 15
remarriage 130, 131
rented housing 105–6, 108–11
repetition of patterns of activity
    see reproduction
repression
  in family 129
  of sexuality 130
  see also oppression
reproduction, social 8, 11–12
'restricted patriarchal nuclear
    family' 120
revenue of state and economy
    76–8
revolutions
  American 4, 88
  Chinese 90
  French 4–5, 36, 88, 90
  industrial 5–6, 15, 60
  labour movements 52
  modern state and 87–91
  Russian 89, 90
  socialist 158
  'two great' 4–9, 16, 88
Rex, J. 103, 105–9, 111
rights
  bargaining 27, 32, 39, 51, 53,
    55
  development of 52–5
  legal 52–4
  political and civil 16, 17, 32,
    37, 39, 51–5, 79, 86
  in traditional societies 21
  see also equality
Rogers, B. 121
Roman Empire 140